IN PARENTS WE TRUST

IN PARENTS WE TRUST

Written by

Karrol M. Karlin

A 1st books.com book
Bloomington, Indiana

ISBN 1-58721-190-4

Cover Design by K.C. McClain

Published by 1stbooks.com
2511 W. Third St., Suite 1
Bloomington, Indiana

ORDER BOOK FROM: www.1stbooks.com

Printed in the United States of America

All proceeds with the exception of ten thousand dollars for
partial recovery of legal fees, will go towards
THE CHILDREN'S RIGHT'S COUNCIL.

1stBooks-rev.04/13/00

ABOUT THE BOOK

In Parents We Trust tells a story regarding a case of false allegations of abuse. Imagine Gerald Karlin's predicament. The father in the story files for continued liberal visitation rights with his two sons. Instead, when the court system finally reinstates visitation, only then does the Karlin family's worst nightmare begin.

After reuniting and spending a happy Father's Day together in June of 1993, he returns the boys to their mother. Soon after, other than court appearances, Karlin wonders if he will ever see his sons again. In fact, he worries if he will lose not only his sons but also his freedom, simply because of a lie. See for yourself, the tragic injustice which the Karlin family must live through while trying to survive a cruel attack by a false weapon and the devastating turn of events which follow.

FOR ALL THE INNOCENT VICTIMS,
ESPECIALLY GERALD, TODD, AND GERRY

BASED ON A TRUE STORY

FOREWORD

The title of this book could just as easily be "Guilty Until Proven Innocent," or "The Injustices of the American Justice System." Ignored and un-helped by those assigned to look after the welfare of children, Karlin portrays what it is like to be caught in a web of biased judicial and human service systems flawed by weaknesses and faults. A loving father, Gerald, has been falsely accused with a hideous crime, the sexual molestation of his two sons. His ex-wife files the accusations with the police long after Gerald begins family court litigation to regain his liberal visitation rights back.

It is an all too familiar story. Karlin's story involves children from divorced parents caught in the middle. But like hundreds, if not thousands of unpublicized similar cases with teachers and child-care workers, it often begins with a simple telephone call. Although many victimized children do suffer the horror of abuse, in other situations, subtle suggestions or overt coercion by an entrusted parent/guardian misleads a child into either playing along or actually believing he/she has been abused. The twisted process, in these cases, ends up hurting the very children the system is supposed to protect, in addition to ruining the lives of innocent adults.

Gerald ends up in jail and has to borrow money to cover his bond. The couple is forced to move due to the mounting family and criminal lawyer's fees. But the lawyers don't seem to help much. Nothing is accomplished in the father's lengthy fight for modification of visitation rights. One criminal lawyer's main interest seems to be money. And the lawyer who is finally supposed to defend Gerald appears so contradictory and evasive, one would think that he is a member of the prosecution. He delays taking action, doesn't return phone calls or letters and pays little or no attention to Gerald or his wife Karrol.

Everything seems to go wrong, one disaster after another. Karrol's father turns ill. Their car's windshield is shattered and must be replaced requiring money the couple does not have. Even the weather is against them. But life goes on.

Yet, Gerald and Karrol are fortunate. They have the love and support of each other and the trust of relatives and friends. On occasion, as a result of the pressures they are under, they find themselves bickering. But, like their belief in God and American justice, which sometimes falters, they always manage to restore their faith and trust in each other and the hope that all will work out well, eventually.

Readers who find themselves or friends or relatives being falsely accused of child abuse will find comfort in knowing that they are not alone in this crazy, mixed-up world. In addition, Karlin provides clues as to how to confront the problems and frustrations encountered.

Does the story end happily? Don't count on it. Remember you are dealing with a system that is out of control.

ROBERT L. EMANS, Ph.D.
Tennessee State University
Nashville, Tennessee

AUTHOR'S NOTE

To expect words to describe or explain a tragedy seems unfair, especially when victims/survivors still feel numb from disbelief, cruel loss and ultimate heartbreak. The best anyone can do is try to heal, remember the good times and adapt to reality, as harsh or indifferent as it may be. Because losing today due to some past misery or injustice serves no purpose.

Though we may learn and teach from the past, within yesterday's fond memories and todays and tomorrows, that is where the hope lies. So in honor of future hope, truth and justice, I offer the following. First, Emerson's wisdom, then my opinion.

> *"Nothing, Falsehood, may indeed stand as the great night or shade on which as a background the living universe paints itself forth; But no FACT is begotten by it; IT CANNOT WORK, FOR IT IS NOT."*

Ralph Waldo Emerson

> *"In this day and age of categorical denials, let those who hold the truth upon their hearts, the facts within their pasts, join the ranks of the falsely accused. For liars, with intent to harm or partakers who choose to cover up rather than act properly to discover the truth; if that defines you, turn about face or stand before the dark canvas 'shade' of inaction and nothingness."*

Karrol M. Karlin

ACKNOWLEDGMENTS

To God, for never giving up on us and restoring our faith, thank you. We know it's supposed to be the other way around. The same to Dr. "Cobers" for everything.

Words cannot express what it meant to have loving family members and true friends offer support during turbulent times, because although both my husband and I admit to flaws and imperfections, we were good, loving parents to Todd and Gerry, nothing less. Without your love and support, "drowning" in the wrongness seemed imminent.

I owe a great deal to my literary friends who inspired me for years. Their reminders of the beauty and purpose of writing helped me to persist.

Lee Shore Literary Agency also drilled into my heart and mind the importance of "persistence and resilience." The phenomenal guidance I received from various staff members at the agency and Sterling and Davidson's advisory book made publication of IN PARENTS WE TRUST possible.

Special thanks to "Tony" from Lee Shore for connecting, offering some editorial assistance and helping me write a better book.

To Dr. Robert L. Emans, your support and willingness to jump in and provide a foreword was a turning point. Your work dealing with the issues of sexual abuse, real or fabricated, is vital to assuring that innocent victims receive the proper help.

I needed some advice. Mr. "Williams," your legal expertise made me feel more secure and helped to avoid certain pitfalls. Thank you so much.

To Vivian at Nerd World, your critical eye and positive feedback always uplifts me. Again, great job!

For the "says it all" cover design, thanks to K.C. McClain for his artistry. I hope my last touches did not distort your work too much.

For my husband's love, strength, courage and grace under fire and my stepsons' lively spirits, this book is for you. May your hearts and bond someday be mended, your future filled with more happy memories together.

Finally, to 1stbooks, located in Bloomington, Indiana, thank you for wandering into my life. I will remain eternally grateful for the opportunity to share our story. We hope increased awareness will spare other innocent children and parents or guardians the life-threatening, tormenting ordeal which ensues due to false allegations of abuse.

Gratefully Yours,
Karrol M. Karlin

CHAPTER 1

I left work a little early and hurried home. Flora, my husband's ex-wife, would be dropping off the kids at the agreed time of five o'clock. As I pulled up in the driveway, Todd and Gerry were alone, standing just inside the door of our small enclosed porch. I turned the motor off and jumped out of the car.

"Hi, you guys, where's your mother?" It was difficult to believe she had left them there and not waited until I got home. The boys were seven and eight, but they showed poor judgment at times, so we rarely left them alone for longer than five minutes.

"I don't know," Todd answered. "She said she had to go somewhere." They both shrugged their shoulders. I unlocked the door and we all stepped inside.

"So how'd it go today, you guys?" I was somewhat anxious to find out the results of their local screening for ADD (attention deficit disorder).

"Okay. They asked me too many questions though," Todd said. He took off his winter jacket and tossed it on the chair.

"I don't know, I didn't do it," Gerry explained.

"You didn't, huh, why not?" I asked but only received a shrug. They were eager to go play in their room, so I dropped the subject. I called their mother to let her know they were okay. The answering machine at a second number, the boy's grandfather's house, intercepted my message, since she was not at home.

"Hey Todd, Gerry, your Dad will be home pretty soon and we're gonna eat spaghetti tonight. How's that sound?" I asked as I stood by the doorway.

"Good. I like your spaghetti. You cook good," Gerry complimented. Todd continued to play.

"Well thanks Gerry. Did you two bring your uniforms for tomorrow's game?" After dodging a few toys, I picked up Todd's backpack and began to unzip it.

"Yeah, yeah we did, we got 'em." Todd stopped trying to handcuff Gerry long enough to look up and give me one of his sweet smiles.

"Hey, do you know where the keys are to those handcuffs, before you go playing sheriff and lock your brother up?" I stroked the top of his head. "Do you?"

"I got it right here in my pocket." He reached in his back pocket to prove it.

"Oh, all right. Good. Well I'm going to go start supper."

I chopped up an onion and green pepper and sautéed them both in an iron skillet, then added the ground beef. After boiling some water, I snapped a pound of spaghetti in half and threw it in to cook.

As I set the table, I could hear the boys. I love the way they light up the house, our family, with such animation and humor. Most of the time they act like such good buddies. They're lucky to have each other, I thought to myself. They seem so different. Todd is the thin one. He has his dad's nose. It turns down and in just at the tip. He exhibits an innate high energy level and continually struggles with the problems it creates. Little Gerry is shorter, stocky, one year older and sports a head of hair twice as coarse as his brother's. He also seems to have a little more sense of direction, certainly calmness. He doesn't look as much like his father, but I can see the resemblance.

After Gerald got home, we all sat down to eat supper.

"My teacher, Mrs. Grazelli, says I'm reading better than Philip, this kid in my class, he got in trouble today 'cause he couldn't sit down and so, um, he just kept gettin' up and so he had to stand out in the hall." Todd rambled on about his day in school.

"Okay Todd, take another bite. Then you can talk for another ten minutes." Gerald encouraged him to eat.

"That's good, your reading is improving," I said.

"Yeah and I'm doin' good too," Gerry chimed in.

"Good, Gerry. You too? Did you have a good day?" I asked.

"Uh huh." He didn't elaborate, but took another bite of food.

I wondered if he had followed through with his reading project, so I asked if he showed his teacher the list of books he had read.

"Yep. And she thought I did good to read all them." He sounded so proud.

"You boys are doing better then. That's what I like to hear. Keep up the good work." Gerald often gave the boys fatherly "pep talks," some lengthier than others. Gerald must have forgotten about the ADD testing. I decided to wait and speak to him after supper about it and the issue about the boys being dropped off at the doorstep and left alone.

But before we finished supper we did discuss what we would do later. It was unanimous, a game of Monopoly. And Todd made it perfectly clear that he wanted to play the real game, not the junior one.

Little Gerry said he wanted to play but suddenly remembered a promise Gerald had made about something else.

"Member, Dad, Karrol got us that big bag of army men from the dollar store and you said next time we come over you'd play." His eyes begged for a yes. I guess Monopoly was a second best activity choice.

"Okay, okay, Ger-Bear. We'll play. Now go on, wash those sticky hands."

"All right! Yes!" He gestured with his little fist clenched and elbow flexed. Then he ran for the bathroom.

Gerald helped me put away a few things in the refrigerator and clean off the plates. Then I took over while he and the boys got out the soldiers and tanks. By seven-thirty Todd was whining because he was knocked out of the Monopoly game. Gerald finally won and we all settled down to watch a movie before going to bed.

I awoke at eight A.M. The boys were wide awake already. I love Saturday mornings with the kids. Nothing like a marathon of Loony Toons to set the mood. After a bowl of Corn Flakes and a good-bye I headed for the store, while the boys were engrossed with the cartoons and Ger slept in.

As I returned from the store, I paused before walking toward the kitchen while holding two bags of heavy groceries stuffed in plastic bags.

"Hi. How are you guys doing?" But there was no response, only silence. The intensity kids watch cartoons with, it's scary. Todd, especially, his fixed stare looks strong enough to burn a whole through the television screen.

After two more unanswered hellos, I set the groceries down, grabbed the remote and clicked off the television. A loud, attentive duet of "Hi" from both of them finally appeased me.

By mid-morning, Gerald and the kids huddled around the coffee table in the living room, and basketball became the important topic of the day. Gerald wore his grey sweats and red YMCA T-shirt; the boys were in their uniform team shirts and black shorts.

Gerald drilled Todd and Gerry. "Well boys, we're gonna play the Magic Marbles today, do you know where you're supposed to be?"

"Yeah, I'm playin' guard," Todd quickly answered.

"Okay. Then what's your job, Todd?" Ger asked as he played the role of coach.

It sounded like he knew just what to do. "I bring the ball down to the basket, uh, then if I have a open shot, I shoot it. If I don't got one I would pass the ball." He looked at his dad for a satisfactory response.

"Yeah and maybe you'll pass it to me this time so I can make the basket." Little Gerry poked Todd in the shoulder as he frowned. Gerald quickly got their attention before it escalated. The pep talk went on and on. Ger reiterated the same game tactics over and over. The idea was to remain focused, watch the ball and of course, "guard you man."

Just before leaving for the game, the boys put on their knee-high athletic socks, sweat pants, and high top tennis shoes. I had to remind them to comb their hair and zip up since it was the middle of February.

Later that afternoon, the score read 'Dangerous Dragons, twenty. Magic Marbles, six.' Gerry had made a basket for the first time. Todd had managed two. They acted a little big-headed for awhile, but it wore off. They were all happy and I was glad.

After their baths that night, little Gerry opted for the top bunk and Todd climbed into the bottom one.

But I asked, "Don't you guys want a story tonight?"

They yelled out a "Yeah!" and quickly Gerry joined us in the bottom bunk. We set up pillows behind our backs and laid comfortably against the wall while reading a book about a bully, and their favorite, The Empire Strikes Back. Then Gerald came in and helped me tuck them in again.

"Now go to sleep you guys, we'll see you in the morning," their dad said after giving them a couple quick hugs. We switched the light off and went back out to watch some more television.

While lying in bed later, I decided to tell Ger about the boys being left on the porch. And I reminded him to ask Flora tomorrow how the ADD screening turned out.

After another enjoyable Sunday morning with the boys, we returned them to their mother. As Gerald came back to the car, I asked what Flora said about the testing on Friday. But he said he didn't feel like talking about it with her today or confronting her about just dropping off the kids. "I'll call her tomorrow." After a couple of days, Ger called to inquire about the test results of Todd and why little Gerry didn't get a chance to complete the screening.

"What?" Gerald's voice sounded like a mixture of surprise and irritation. "So he's there now?" He seemed stunned.

"Who's where?" I knew something was wrong. Gerald held up his finger to tell me to wait a minute. He just kept saying, "hmm," and acting more puzzled and concerned as he listened. "Okay. Bye." Then he sat down and stared.

"Well, what's going on," I prodded. "What's wrong, are Todd and Gerry all right?"

"I guess Todd's in the hospital in Clover City, in the psych unit over there." Ger kept staring, trying mentally to figure it out. His eyes blinked regularly about every two seconds.

"What? What happened? I don't understand. They were just here. They were fine all weekend." I sat down by Gerald on the sofa.

Oh God, now what, I thought. It was always one thing after another with Flora. For the last three and a half years we had managed somehow to raise the kids on a part-time basis, juggling them back and forth between the two households, but sometimes it was not easy.

I suppose we experienced frustrations and difficulties similar to many marriages who have to deal with an ex-spouse in order to jointly raise children. Occasionally we would go over to pick the boys up as planned and nobody was home. That was aggravating. Equally frustrating for Flora, I suppose, were several times when Gerald was supposed to pick up the boys and he had decided to drink instead. I know this was disappointing to Todd and Gerry.

Although for a while things seemed to be going fairly well. The boys had adjusted. Flora and Gerald communicated as needed regarding matters with the kids. Apparently their divorce was not an amicable one, but it certainly seemed like something in the past, that everyone had moved on with their lives. Flora was remarried now too. Recently, however, she was acting strange, wanting more control over the kids. It was my guess that her husband didn't like the idea of having to deal with Gerald, or having to raise someone else's kids since they now had two children of their own. And sometimes Todd and Gerry would attempt to use certain tactics on their mother in my presence, like saying something to the effect that "Dad and Karrol always takes us somewhere, why don't you?" I'd try to explain that their mom has two other little kids so it's harder to get out. I know Todd and Gerry's ploys did not set well with Flora, but they were just being kids.

"Well, what's going on?" I begged for more information."

"I don't know. Flora says they wanted to put Todd in right away Friday after the test, that he was so bad. She said he's been talking to himself, talking about killing himself and just acting so bad lately. He's up all night tossing and turning." Ger shrugged his shoulders.

6

"But he was fine. What the heck is she talking about? Has she said anything like this before now?"

"No. No, this is the first I've heard of this kind of stuff," Ger replied.

Then it occurred to me. "Wait a minute, if he was so bad on Friday, talking suicide or something, then why'd she just drop 'em off here at the doorstep? This is so sad. That poor kid, now what's she up to?" I shook my head in frustration.

"I don't know, Karrol. I don't know what the hell's going on. I have the number to the hospital. Let me call."

He picked up the cordless and dialed.

"Yeah, call. See what's going on. See if he's okay and if we can see him. Tell them he was fine all weekend."

But we soon found out that we could not reach Todd, not even to tell him we loved him, that we were thinking about him and hoped he was okay.

All of a sudden, I realized that a non-custodial father and worse, merely a stepmother, had no rights, none. Flora had not given the okay for Gerald to speak to anyone at the hospital. So by law, supposedly, they could not even admit that Todd was there.

We agonized and could do nothing but wait a whole week, basically beg until Flora decided to concede and inform us of a secret code number which allowed access to Todd. Since she had custodial say so regarding who could have contact, without that number Gerald had no rights to see his own son.

By the time we did see him, it was apparent that whatever chance we had to participate in the health care of Todd, to offer pertinent, accurate information to his well-being while last in our care; that chance to communicate such vital facts was gone. Our input was not welcomed either. All efforts were thwarted and offset by whatever information Flora had wished to provide.

She was back to her old tricks again of trying to cause friction and assign blame toward Gerald. It boiled down to one rule of thumb, if Flora could not get control of Todd while he was in her care, it was unquestionably Gerald's fault. Ger always bit his tongue. He had to, he was being extorted. Retort and she had the power, we wouldn't get to see the kids.

7

By the time we saw Todd in the hospital it was evident Flora was up to something. We stepped into the room and exchanged smiles and hugs with Todd, then sat down. As a staff member stood outside the doorway, we heard her say, "Hey, that has to be supervised. There has to be someone in there at all times." Obeying orders, the Psych Tech hurriedly entered the room.

Gerald and I frowned at each other in bewilderment. No visits were ever supervised, never once, since I had met the kids in 1989, a few years back. We quickly reverted back to visiting with Todd since we knew our time together would be limited.

I noticed he seemed more fidgety than normal and displayed the sullen, dark circles around his eyes which depicts the side effects of a kid on medication. But it was obvious we were all happy to be together. We didn't pry about the situation, just kept the conversation light-hearted. Before leaving, we handed him another cheery card from my family. We had already mailed him one.

Upon departing the hospital, we got no answers from the staff regarding Todd's condition. It was as if they thought we did not exist, we were invisible or something. Yet, in truth, we could have offered so much, to explain how Todd, if offered love and structure, functioned quite well. But for Todd's entire stay Gerald was treated, not like the involved, loving father I had witnessed for the last several years, but like a pest, someone to be ignored or worried about.

Poor Todd. Ger and I felt so badly for him. We knew he needed to be in school since he did have problems there. Now he would experience this setback and probably fall even more behind.

After a few days of contemplation, we thought, maybe they will help him, behaviorally or academically. But we had our doubts, especially since all they would hear would be Flora's one-sided story about Todd. We feared that she would relay only bad, trumped up details of his behavior, nothing good. Maybe it was so, in her care, a kid out of control, starting fires, punching walls. We don't know because we were not there. So often she would describe him as a destructive, hopeless child.

We never witnessed any such thing. We dealt with a creative, certainly high-energy kid with a twinkle in his eye, someone who with guidance and follow-through functioned well and showed great potential. We certainly never saw any signs of a severely emotionally disturbed or severely depressed child.

So often though, Flora would call and leave a message on the answering machine and say, "You need to come and get Todd and do something with him today." Then she would hang up without further explanation. It was never fun to come home to such disheartening messages. We couldn't understand it. It was like we were talking about two different kids.

We wondered and waited to see what was in store for Todd, as well as us, after he returned home. Oddly enough, things returned to normal for awhile. Todd rejuvenated back to his old self, while in our care anyway. The kids played more sports as their dad coached. And we were once again as we so often joked, "The Kar-lin Fam-i-ly!" Two snaps of the fingers followed our singing.

CHAPTER 2

Following Todd's stay in the hospital over in Clover City, the kids followed up with some outpatient therapy with Dr. Tano, a psychiatrist here in town who deals with learning disabilities. Gerald, I, and even Flora knew that Clover City was too far away. We recommended Dr. Tano because we saw her name in the phone book and had read some of her newspaper articles.

The kids maintained a full schedule, school, outpatient therapy and the YMCA. Gerald and I just assumed the idea behind the therapy was to help the boys improve academically, determine if any underlying problems with learning did exist and assist Flora in gaining better control over Todd.

We continued to see the kids often. Sometimes their basketball games were scheduled on Wednesday evenings so they usually spent the night. Throughout the winter months and springtime, weekends continued to be a great deal of fun with the boys. Occasionally Gerald would drive the kids to see the doctor, but again, although he asked to be included more, he was not given the opportunity.

(What we did not know at the time, but is important to interject here to denote the chronological order of events, is that Flora had made an allegation of sexual abuse to one of the therapists at Clover City. She had apparently implied that Ger was sexually abusing Todd. At this time, CPS got involved, but dropped the case when the kids denied any abuse.)

The boys kept coming over and one weekend in July they met their fifteen-year-old half-sister for the first time.

Nikki had grown up in Washington with her mother and older sister, Karley. Everything was exciting and ran smoothly for the first few minutes, before the novelty of a first introduction wore off. But soon enough the three of them were showing their true colors and acting out like any other siblings toward each other.

Gerald had to work quite a bit, but I took a few days off and we kept busy with various interesting activities. The four of us toured Kellton which included a bird's eye view from the Bell Tower and a majestic, serene boat ride. We rented scary movies, popped popcorn and really risked it one night as all of us roller-skated around in circles to music at the skating rink.

One night, I couldn't resist. I whisked them off to my favorite thing to do in the summertime and the kids and I had a great time at the drive-in movie. We picked a good night, it was warm and clear and no pesky bugs bothered us, for some reason.

Sunday morning arrived and we headed for the Y.M.C.A. so Nikki could watch Todd and Gerry's T-Ball game. They won too.

In the afternoon we all sat around at the kitchen table and played cards, Ger included. Since my husband and the kids are Mexican-American, Gerald often played upon their ethnic heritage, although when I tell my friends about Gerald's background, they don't tend to believe me. His mother was a standard mixture of English-American roots and he inherited her lighter complexion and a head of wavy light brown hair that never seems destined to turn grey. I think the hospitable aspect of his personality came from her southern Indiana connections. But his dad, and his grandfather and who knows how far back that half of the family tree goes, originated straight out of Mexico. Ger and the kids could speak the language fairly well too.

"Andale! Andale! Todd. Gerry. Now," their dad yelled. "Quit fooling around and play. And quit bumping the table. Now it's your turn, Gerry."

"Okay. Does Karrol got a two?" He leaned over and peeked at my cards as he made the request.

"Gerry, you're cheating. You can't peek at the cards first," Nikki informed him.

I pulled my cards back.

"Now quit!" Ger yelled.

Little Gerry looked directly at his dad. "Well, she looked at mine," he said innocently.

"No," I explained. "You *showed* me your cards. You *showed* me yours."

He asked if I had an ace and I told him, "No, go fish."

12

"You're lying." It caught us all off guard and we all roared laughing.

The kids went outside in the back yard for awhile after the card game which gave me the opportunity to play mom again by cooking supper.

When the long weekend was over, Todd and Gerry said good-bye to Nikki. I wondered how many years it would be before they saw each other again, probably way too long. On July 19, 1992, Gerald and I accompanied Nikki back home via United Airlines.

Upon arrival at the airport, Grandpa Gerald got to see his adorable three-year-old granddaughter, Jo-Jo, for the second time and finally meet E.J., his bouncy two-year-old grandson, for the first time.

Of course it was great to see Karley again and finally meet Martin, her husband. We only stayed a few days, but had a terrific time visiting, not to mention climbing Mt. Rainier and enjoying the furry creatures, large and small, at Northwest Trek.

We would have had even more fun if the boys had come along. We've been lucky enough to squeeze in the few vacations with them, but nothing out of state.

The hot month of August rolled around and we all experienced a thrilling time on Todd's eighth birthday at an amusement park. All of us were exhausted. We stopped by Flora's on the way home but she wasn't there which meant that the kids would have to get up very early with their dad and be returned in the morning on Gerald's way to work. Before retiring ourselves that night, we gave Todd one last birthday kiss. Little Gerry turned away, like he does sometimes, when I try to kiss him.

We didn't see the boys again until one day in September. Everything appeared to be okay. But when Gerald took them home, Flora began to cry and act strangely again. A little while after Ger returned the phone rang.

I stepped out of the bathroom and couldn't believe my ears. Gerald jolted out of our brown chair in the living room. "Who me? You think I'm having sex with my own two sons, are you crazy or something?"

"Oh my God, no." I mumbled this to myself as I covered my face with my hands.

Then Gerald finally said, "Fine, if you think I hurt the boys then keep them away from me, but I'm telling you right now I did not do anything. So if you think they're being abused, then find out who's doing it fast." He slammed the phone down. He paced and directed his comments toward me. "Now she's saying that the kids have been abused. I don't know, Karrol, I just don't know anymore. She is bound and determined to make my life hell, to see the destruction of me, no matter what." He sighed and finally sat down. "I don't think those kids have showed any signs of abuse, especially sexually abuse, do you?"

"No. No, I don't." I mean, God forbid that they have struggled through some awful sexual abuse ordeal and kept it a secret. But I'm sure we'd notice something. I can't believe this, I mean this is totally bizarre, and it's beginning to frighten me."

"Yeah, tell me about it. You think I'm not scared right now of what she might do next? Well I am. God knows what that woman is capable of." He lit up a cigarette, then remembered his promise, so he went to the kitchen, opened the back door and smoked back there instead.

A little later on we recalled one evening with the boys. The four of us had watched the poignant movie *Radio Flyer*. While Todd sat right next to me on the couch he looked at me and said, "If anybody ever abuses me, I'll just kill 'em." The movie dealt with the physical abuse of a little boy. Todd said it so self-confidently, I believed him. Nobody was going to mess with Todd Karlin and get away with it.

A discussion about abuse and self-defense had followed. Both Ger and I explained how important it is to tell someone, and keep telling until someone listens. We emphasized that nobody should ever want to hurt or kill someone, but if that person is hurting us then we have the right to fight back, to do whatever it takes to get away.

The day after seeing the movie, we remembered Flora calling us. She directed her question to Gerald over the phone, "What is Karrol doing telling Todd that it's all right to kill people?" Gerald explained the movie, and said to her, "The issue was self-defense. Wouldn't you want him to get away if somebody was hurting him?"

We went to bed worrying about things and didn't know what to think. We assumed that we were probably in for some kind of senseless trouble, though. As we digested the shocking statements received from her, and got beyond the point of thinking about ourselves, we began to talk about Todd and Gerry and wondered if they were all right.

We attempted another September visit with the boys. Gerald said he wanted to "straighten this thing out right here and now." But when he called Flora, she not only refused to let the boys visit, she threatened Gerald.

She said, "If you ever want to see these kids again, you'll have to take me to court."

It was difficult to accept the aggravating, unbelievable turn of events, and being denied access again to the kids. We felt so powerless. Gerald had relinquished his custodial rights when he got divorced. He said he would have signed anything to get out of the unhappy marriage. I guess now he was paying for giving up his fatherly rights.

Then Todd entered the hospital again and remained there until the third week in October. We had no way to contact him except by mail. We knew it would still reach Flora, but hoped that he would receive our message of love. I missed taking the boys trick-or-treating that year.

We knew that it might be quite some time before we saw the boys again. Consequently, Gerald planned an appointment with a lawyer. Then something bizarre happened. We called up as usual and spoke to Todd and Gerry and asked about a visit, and Flora consented. It had to be on a Saturday, and unfortunately Gerald was already scheduled to work, so I picked up the kids and spent a rushed, but delightful, two hours with them.

On November 14, 1992, we kept our appointment with the lawyer and Ger filed for modification of visitation rights, since it seemed that visits would continue to be minimized. Contrary to Flora's threats and in the midst of sexual abuse allegations, she did not end visitations.

We continued to see the kids for monthly two-hour visits, sometimes longer, especially one six-hour visit. All visits remained unsupervised. The kids didn't offer any explanations and we didn't prod. They said, "I don't know, she doesn't tell us why, but she says we can't ever spend the night again."

CHAPTER 3

Gerald and I were anxious about walking into a courtroom on March 11, 1993 and finally obtaining our liberal visitation rights back as parents. However, we received a last minute phone call indicating that court was cancelled. Flora was in the hospital and would not be able to make it.

We got through to the kids the next day, because we wondered who was watching them. I heard some background noise. Apparently Flora had just returned from the hospital, so the kids had to hang up.

Although our court date was postponed until May 3, Todd and little Gerry came over one day in late March and ended up staying longer than usual which was a treat. I thought it was kind of odd the way the four of us seemed to always pick up where we left off and managed to enjoy some quality time together. Yet it certainly didn't feel right, missing so much time with them. They offered no explanations. And we did not press them.

As we got dressed, we remained on edge due to the anticipation once again about a scheduled morning in court. We were almost out the door when the phone rang.

Gerald answered. "Hello. Yes. Hmm. But... But can't they set a date up right away since we've had to wait so long? This is really getting ridiculous, one cancellation after another."

I wondered how he could keep his voice so calm.

"Tell her we would like our day in court."

I gritted my teeth. The situation was beginning to feel hopeless, like we would never get the chance to step foot in court.

Gerald hung up the phone and explained the reason for the postponement, all the while trying to console me as I paced, cried and spouted off about the futility of it all.

"This is awful. We're never gonna get our day in court. Okay the judge's mother died, don't they have substitutes to sit in for this kind of thing?" We sympathized with anyone who had just lost a mother. We both knew what it felt like. But we were so bewildered again by the inability to move forward. We just couldn't get anywhere.

"I tried to press her for a speedy court date, hon, but I guess she's at the mercy of the legal system just as much as we are." He sighed. We walked into the living room. "She said she'd call with the next date as soon as she gets one."

"Yeah, and then what's going to happen? This is so unfair. It's just not right, you having to wait so long to see your own kids."

I looked into Gerald's green eyes and detected the same sadness and frustration I was feeling. But he always seemed to handle things better than me, one day at a time, one setback at a time.

"Well, we'll just have to wait, honey, there's nothing else we can do." We embraced briefly, then began to discuss what we might be able to accomplish throughout the day since now we had a full day without plans.

On June 14, 1993 we took the phone off the hook and decided to show up as planned, no matter what. We parked and waited in the car on the east side of the Little City Courthouse red brick building. Our mixed feelings of hoping for something productive to occur and ultimately harboring skepticism were contradictory.

"I'll just wait in the car. If anything substantial really looks like it's going to happen, you can come and get me," I said as I began to lean back and get comfortable.

"Oh no. You're coming with me. Kathleen said she wanted you there too."

He talked me into it. We never stepped inside a courtroom, only a hallway, but we did make some progress and for that we were very happy. As we sat on the bench and waited, our lawyer walked back and forth between us and Flora's lawyer.

Kathleen informed us, "What I'm going for here is simply your regular divorce situation visitation rights. And with your particular situation, a phasing-in schedule has been suggested, you know, to give the kids a chance to adjust again. So just to take it a little bit slower at first." Flora's lawyer came around the corner and called Kathleen back to the conference room.

We grew restless as we waited. Gerald began to pace as I struck up a conversation with a friendly couple who sounded like they were going through some type of family court turmoil involving their children too. We exchanged phone numbers and promised to call each other sometime.

After going downstairs so he could smoke a cigarette, Gerald returned. I introduced him quickly because I noticed that the other couple's attorney was walking toward them.

Finally our lawyer came back out and sat down beside us on the bench. She showed us something on paper that looked pretty good. Kathleen referred to it as the phasing-in schedule that she had mentioned.

"Here's what we have in the proposal. You can start on Father's Day with a twelve-hour visit, then every Saturday and eventually the kids will be spending every other weekend with you, plus every other holiday." She paused and waited for Gerald's response. As she sat in the middle of us it dawned on me that she was such a petite lady, even shorter than me. Her soft-spoken voice and the good news began to have a tranquilizing effect on me.

Ger and I looked at each other like we wanted to exchange a high-five or something, but just continued to listen. Unfortunately, the next thing we heard got us all riled up again.

"Now I just want to make you aware that Flora did mention to her lawyer that she is still concerned about the abuse issue."

I retorted, "Yeah, what abuse issue, the one in her head?" I sat there knowing without a doubt that this was not an abuse issue, but a divorce issue. I let Gerald interject, because I knew if I carried on, I would get too upset.

"Well I hope she's checking out everyone that's been around the boys lately then, if she really thinks they've been abused, because I'll tell you right now, I know I didn't do anything to my kids."

Kathleen just sat there quietly. She didn't know what to say.

Then I had to add the obvious. "Well, I just have one thing to say, if she is so concerned about the kids and pointing the finger at Ger here, then why does she keep sending her kids back to their father, the alleged abuser? I just don't understand.

Seriously, does that make any sense at all?" I awaited her response to a direct question.

"No. No it doesn't make sense. That's probably why she's trying to stop visitation, because she knows that people will start asking the same question." She stood up as she saw Flora's lawyer come around the corner.

Gerald and I glanced at each other. I decided to try and get the good feeling back. "Hey, just in time for Father's Day. We got 'em back, sweetheart. Things are beginning to move in our direction again. I think we'll have a picnic, what do you think?" I asked enthusiastically.

"Sounds okay to me. I just hope we don't have any more trouble. Did she say the whole day, for Father's Day?"

"That's what she said."

We smiled at each other as we both decided to stand up and walk around a little.

When we got home, I typed up the new schedule and stuck it on the refrigerator. Gerald and I felt great for the rest of the day. Good timing, I thought, just in time for Father's Day.

The big day arrived. But it was just our luck, Gerald had received his work schedule before we knew anything about getting the kids back, so he had to work all night. I decided to let him sleep in as long as possible.

I let Kassy, Gerald's other teenage daughter, sleep in too. Raised in the south, just like her grandmother, she reminded me so much of her. It would be a rare chance for the boys and Kassy to get together.

Sometimes I sit and say to myself, does Ger really have five children? People are actually grandparents at forty? But that was always one of the best things about our marriage. I had always wanted kids, but never seemed to settle down to do anything about it. But with Ger in my life, especially from the first moment I met Todd and Gerry, I knew it was a package deal, instant kids. Not that we didn't all have to get to know each other, one by one.

The first thing in the morning, I cooked the Sloppy Joe mixture and left it warming in the slow-cooker. Then I placed a chocolate cake in the oven. At about 8:35 A.M., I called and let little Gerry know they could expect me about ten minutes late.

As soon as the cake was done, I hurried over to pick up the kids. I parked in front of where they lived and honked. Usually they came running out, but since they didn't, I went up the stairs to their apartment door and knocked. I could hear the kids talking loudly.

"I'm here; are they ready?" I asked Flora as she opened the door. I wasn't sure how to act toward Flora with all that had been going on, so I did my best to act like nothing was going on.

Todd ran up to me with a mouth full of cereal and tried to say hi.

"I guess you guys didn't hear my horn, huh?"

He shook his head, no. I saw Gerry come around the corner. He didn't have any socks on.

Flora explained that she thought I wasn't coming until about ten. I realized the word ten must have confused Gerry when I said ten minutes after nine.

As they jumped in the car I told them how glad I was to see them. Then, at their request, I turned the radio to their favorite music station.

"Hey, you guys, we're gonna have an old-fashioned picnic today. You like Sloppy Joes?" I looked in the rearview mirror to see if I could see Gerry.

"Yeah, I like 'em," Gerry answered.

"Uh huh, I do too." Todd started to turn up the radio but I caught him just in time.

"It's loud enough. Okay?"

"Okay." He leaned back.

"Oh, I forgot to ask your mom, are we dropping you off back here later? Or did your mom say something else about dropping you off?" I glanced at Todd, but Gerry quickly answered.

"Yeah. My mom didn't tell me nothing."

While we drove toward Bear Lake, I let the kids know that some of my family was coming to the picnic too and how much their dad was looking forward to seeing them, and how Kassy couldn't wait to see them either.

21

But it was like old times, the boys and I having the opportunity to take off and go for a walk. So I took advantage of the opportunity. Besides Ger needed at least another hour of sleep.

Oddly enough, the one morning I came prepared to feed the begging seagulls, they were no where in sight. The water felt tolerable and the sun had begun to shine already, so after some coaxing the boys jumped into the lake water. I forgot to mention swim trunks so their blue-jean cut-offs served the purpose.

Gerry and Todd acted so carefree while they enjoyed the water, like they didn't have a care in the world.

Gerald woke up right away as the kids ran into the house, right into the bedroom and started shouting, "Hi, Dad." He began to prioritize: hugs, coffee, and cigarettes.

It was great to see the three of them together again as they sat at the kitchen table. Gerald asked if they had eaten their breakfast and they said yes. Then Kassy walked in and Gerald began to reacquaint the three of them.

The kids grew anxious to spend time in their room and run around in the back yard, so Gerald decided to take a shower. "Hey Gerry, let's go get somethin' to take outside."

"Be careful with Kassy's stuff in there, okay. Kassy, you put up anything breakable, all right?" I warned her.

"Oh I will, believe me. C'mon, you guys."

I got busy in the kitchen frosting the cake.

Gerry came back in. "Hey Karrol, where's Tiger?"

"Oh, he's in the backyard on his chain. You wanna go see him and say hi, go ahead." I opened the back screen door and let Gerry out.

The clock said noon. Only another half hour, I thought. I did a rush job on cleaning the kitchen, then took my Charlie Chaplin T-shirt off and replaced it with a short-sleeved blue and white paisley blouse.

I sat down for a minute on the couch and wondered if I had time to vacuum. The humidity was building up already, so I turned the fan setting on top of the television on medium. Another hot, muggy day was in the forecast.

One by one my family started to arrive. We thought about inviting Ger's sisters from Kellton, but we knew they probably didn't want to make the drive in the heat.

The boys acted somewhat shy at first since they hadn't seen everyone, dad, Katie and my brothers for awhile. But as soon as they started rough-housing with Jonathan things felt like normal again.

"Whoa, wait, stop you two, you can't jump like that with Jon on there too." Gerald explained that if they wanted to jump on the trampoline they would have to make sure Jonathan was clear of it. A friend had given me a small three-foot-wide trampoline a long time ago and the boys loved it.

"So, Gerald, you won in court then yesterday, Karrol was telling us." My brother Perry and his wife sat across from Gerald and I at the picnic table.

"I guess that's what happened. I'm supposed to get them now on Saturdays and pretty soon weekends again. That's what my lawyer said yesterday." He reached for another hamburger bun.

"We have 'em all day today. I promised to go on a bike ride with them later. I wonder how long they're going to let me hold off. You want some more potato salad, Dad?" I offered.

"Nope, I'm fine. I'm full. I can't eat that much any more at one time for some reason." He took his baseball hat off and wiped his forehead with a napkin.

"It's getting hot out here isn't it, Dad," Katie said.

"A little bit. I'll have some more of that lemonade, Karrol. That'll quench my thirst and cool me off a bit." He looked over and saw the kids playing near the back fence. "The boys look like they're having fun. I'll bet you're glad that's all over with, Gerald."

"Yes Sir, I sure am."

It turned out to be a terrific day. After all of the family visiting, food, fun, and bike ride with the boys, I began to straighten up the kitchen while Gerald settled down to watch a baseball game. It was still daylight out, so we let the kids play outside awhile longer. They had a few friends that always came by to see them whenever they were here visiting. I took a peek

23

and found them playing catch in the alley. It was funny, the boys weren't interested in the game, but Kassy sat and watched it with Gerald.

Then he looked at the clock and decided to call Flora and tell her he was on his way. But there was no answer at either place.

"You tried their grandfather's too?" I asked.

"Yes. There's no answer anywhere." He began to get irritated. "I'm thinking about the court order. I don't want to get into any trouble because I'm five minutes late or something." He dialed again.

"Well," I tried to point out, "you can't take them home until somebody's home. Hopefully she'll call or we'll just have to keep calling." This type of thing was not unusual. In fact, we had learned to expect it, long ago.

The phone finally rang. After hanging up, Gerald explained that Flora acted upset.

"Upset, why should she be upset?" I asked.

"I don't know. She just said, 'Well, where's the kids?' You heard me tell her I've been calling, right?" He went to the back door and yelled for the boys to come in.

As they came running in I checked to make certain two baseball mitts and one ball were accounted for.

"You guys have to go?" Kassy asked.

"Yeah, but we get to go fishin' Saturday, right Dad?" Gerry wanted to double-check next week's plans.

"That's right. I'll pick you up at nine in the morning on Saturday. Now say good-bye to your sister." He gave little Gerry a nudge toward her.

"All right," he whined. Then enthusiastically he said, "See you later, alligator."

We all exchanged several good-byes and of course I had to get my hugs in. Then as usual, I stood at the doorway and waved good-bye. And they were gone.

When Ger returned, he told me more about the phone call and how when he dropped the kids off, Flora was acting weird again.

"I don't know, Karrol," Ger said, "she says she was waiting outside for the boys, that she told Gerry to tell us to pick 'em up

24

at their grandfather's house. She says she was waiting out front. She acted like I was trying to pull something by not bringing them home right away." He took his baseball hat off and hung it on a rack by the door, then sat down on the couch and tried to focus again on the game.

"Well, I asked Gerry this morning if she told him anything different as far as where to drop them off, besides home and he said no. Besides, I had to go up the stairs today and knock. She could have told me then. Just don't let her get to you, honey, it's not worth it."

"Okay." He let out a sigh. "Whatever. So, Kass, what's the score, have you been following it for me?" He put her on the spot.

"No, Dad, I don't know. Sorry," she apologized.

I decided to lie on my bed and watch a movie, while they finished watching the game. I reflected on the day with Dad, everyone else and the kids. They were back in our lives and it felt great. But for how long, I wondered?

This morning in the car, I told Todd and Gerry how things would be back to normal soon, how they could come over more now again and eventually spend weekends like before. How their mother and Ger and I worked things out. They seemed very happy and relieved.

On the following Saturday, as planned, Ger called to let Flora know he would be coming by soon to pick up the kids.

"What are you talking about?" I heard him say. He looked at me and started shaking his head, no. I knew it meant more trouble and heartache. "I'm supposed to be able to get the kids today, Flora." He made one last ditch effort to reason with her as well as remind her of the court decision the other day.

I sat down in the brown chair and realized that another day was about to be ruined. Gerald was hurting emotionally. He retreated to the kitchen so he could smoke. The old feeling of hopelessness began to sink in again. It amazed me, the way he could always bite his tongue though, refrain from shouting or cursing at her. He had to, in the past so many times, hold back any sort of confrontation on any matter, any firing back at all. Retort, and he knew he would not be able to see the kids.

25

We have tried to cooperate, I thought to myself. Why is she doing this?

"Ger, what did she say?" I said loud enough so he could hear me.

He stepped back into the living room. "You want to know what she said? She said, 'You're not getting the kids. Talk to your lawyer.' That's what she said."

"So now we can't go fishing with them." I stood up and could sense myself getting angrier by the minute. "That's it, this is the last straw. I'm calling the police." I walked over and picked up the telephone.

"Yes," my voice cracked. "We have a court order to see our kids today. We were supposed to pick them up and we just called and their mother is saying we can't see them."

"You say you have papers?" the officer asked.

"Yes, we just went to court. We have papers."

"Then bring the papers and give us the address and we'll meet you there in fifteen minutes," he explained.

When I told Gerald though, he adamantly refused to put the kids through some parental "tug of war." "Fine, if you're not going to fight when we have the law on our side finally, then I've had it, you're on your own from now on." I walked into our bedroom and slammed the door behind me on purpose.

A few minutes later Gerald had a change of heart. He checked the court documents. But there were no signatures.

We found out by the police and our lawyer's assistant, who was in the office to answer our questions that morning, that the unsigned proposal was worth about the same as a wallet filled with counterfeit money. In other words, it was useless. It made no sense. When we learned that a judge had not even been present that last day in court, the whole mess irritated us even more so. We thought the sole purpose for canceling the previous court date was because the judge could not attend.

We tried our best to forget about it all for Kassy's sake and enjoy our day at Wooden Lake. But it was easier said than done. We did try out the paddleboat as promised. But Gerald and I were both preoccupied, frustrated and angry. We felt like we were starting back at square one with the visitation matter. And we didn't really even know what we were dealing with in relation to Flora's accusations against Gerald.

It became more and more difficult to believe that things would return to normal any time soon.

CHAPTER 4

The situation escalated and became more frightening. We were caught off guard by the next incident because we had just returned from a pleasant, relaxing weekend in mid July. On a trip down south to return Kassy, we had camped on the way down and on the way back at a KOA in Kristopher, Indiana.

We were home ten minutes and the phone rang.

"Hello. Can I speak to a Gerald Karlin?" the authoritative male voice asked politely.

"May I ask who's calling?" For some reason I had a feeling it was a policeman. I gave Gerald a pensive look as I walked toward him.

"Yes, this is Detective Kurk from the police station."

"Okay, he's right here." I handed the phone to Ger and shrugged.

Apparently the detective explained that Flora had brought the kids in and Todd and Gerry had made statements saying that Gerald had sexually abused them over a period of several years.

Without hesitating, Gerald answered to the claims. "Yeah, I'll make a statement right now. I didn't do it. I'm innocent. This is all coming from a court visitation battle that's been going on for some time." He asked the detective if he wanted to see the papers and court documents.

The detective expressed doubts and inconsistencies about the kids' statements, but informed Gerald that he had to report it to the prosecutor's office in Crestwood Edge.

Gerald called our lawyer and was advised not to make any further statements, but we had second thoughts the next day. We thought maybe if the officer would at least look at the stack of court papers we had collected and the proposal of agreed visitation recently granted which Flora had reneged on after one visit, the whole thing would be dropped.

Unfortunately the detective had gone to Crestwood Edge to take care of something. We knew it was this matter with Gerald and the kids.

The next day we called him again.

"Well, they're not going straight up with it," he informed me.

"Straight up, what's that mean?" I asked.

"It means there will be a hearing. You can take it to the people, let them decide. That's what I told them. Let's take it to the people. You'll have a chance to tell your side." He spoke gruffly in distinct tones. He sounded friendly though, like he was on our side.

"So you had something to do with that," I said, "getting a hearing, because they have to see this isn't true. If she's got Todd and Gerry making statements like this, then she's got to be doing something to make them say it because I know it just isn't true."

"Well, like I said, some things just didn't sound right, but there will be a hearing, then they'll decide if there is cause to pursue an indictment or not. So that's all I can tell you for now." He hinted that he had to hang up.

"Thank you, Detective Kurk," I said, "but one more thing. My husband Gerald told me to ask you if there is ever any kind of warrant for his arrest, if you would please just call him and he would walk in." I passed along my husband's request.

After saying good-bye, I hung up the phone, sat down, and began to feel the magnitude of the situation. This isn't happening, this just cannot be happening, I thought over and over to myself.

Later that evening as I spoke with Gerald, we both felt some relief since it seemed like the detective doubted Flora's accusations and the boys' statements, and we would have a chance to tell our side, the truth. But in the meantime, as it all sunk in, it became more clear. Our life as we knew it was quickly being turned upside down. I think we both began to suffer from underlying rage, and did not know what to do about it.

For a while all I thought about were the what ifs. What if they actually arrest Ger for this? What if he goes to jail? What if we can't get Todd and Gerry back? And I thought, God, what if she would have accused me too?

Both Gerald and I wondered how this could be allowed to happen. All anybody had to do was to take a few minutes to listen to our side of the story, and be informed of the sequence of things. These claims were filed eight months after Ger had begun his fight to get liberal visitation with the kids back. Finally he gets his day in court, wins his rights back, and after one visit, Flora and the kids end up at the police station saying these awful things.

Most of all though, what didn't make sense was the fact that she kept sending the kids back over to visit. Even Father's Day. Court proposal or not, Gerald and I both expressed the same sentiment one day as we thought about how ridiculous it was. If we thought someone was abusing the boys like this, we wouldn't care one iota what took place in court, we'd run away before returning the kids to someone we believed was sexually abusing them.

One thing became clear. There is no such honorable thing as innocent until proven guilty. From the onset of the initial filing of allegations, a loving father who had begun a legal fight to assure the right to see his kids, now had to fight not only sexual abuse allegations, but also a bureaucratic system which seemed biased against him from the very beginning. Of course we worried about what would become of Todd and Gerry. Would any of us ever get our "real" lives back?

After a spell of disbelief and letting fear and anger overwhelm us, common sense kicked in. Gerald ordered, "Call Child Protective Services. Tell them what's going on. They should be able to help us and the kids." He went to the kitchen and searched the yellow pages for the number. "Will you call?"

"Sure. Give me the number." I dialed and asked to speak to the person in charge. "Yes, Mrs. Arland, my name is Karrol Karlin and I need to talk to you about an awful situation. We need your help and our kids need your help." I proceeded to tell her the whole story. Gerald sat at the table next to me listening.

Fighting back tears, I explained the whole ordeal and asked what she could do. To my surprise she seemed to be aware of Todd and Gerry as two children in need of services.

"Well, Mrs. Karlin," she answered, "we're aware of Todd and Gerry's situation and the kids are getting counseling." There was a tinge of compassion in her voice but I wondered if she had heard anything I just said.

"Oh really, counseling for what?" I questioned. "Don't you realize what I've just explained to you? Aren't you going to check into the truth at all, to what we're telling you is really happening here? Please Mrs. Arland, those kids need help and they need it now," I pleaded.

There was only silence, no sign of a response to my pleas for help. I composed myself somewhat, then began to speak again. "Okay, okay, please listen just for a second."

"I'm listening," she said.

"Now why would a mother continue to send her kids to their father if she thought he was sexually abusing them? Because that's what she kept doing. Don't you think that's strange?" I awaited her response which I was certain would be a yes.

"No."

"Yes, you do. You must!" I tried to convince her how she had to feel. I thought, who wouldn't think it was bizarre, at least neglectful behavior?

"No, because the kids never said a name before, they wouldn't name him." She explained her reasoning. She shocked me again. "Oh yes, oh yes, named or not by the kids, it was alleged a long time ago that she thought Gerald was abusing the kids. Not only that, but she could have had the kids supervised and never once did she pursue that. She just kept sending them along." I informed her of some facts.

The C.P.S. woman did not concede or offer to help. Feeling defeated, I hung up. Shortly after we became aware of the allegations, I contacted VOCAL (Victims of Child Abuse Laws) in Colorado. While in college, I had listened to a single adoptive father speak one day in class. He had suffered through a sad ordeal of false sexual abuse charges which compelled him to found VOCAL.

The chapter representatives offered support, sent literature and gave us the number and address of a chapter located in St. Rosalie, closer to home. We contacted that chapter too, in the hopes of making the two-hour drive some day to participate in their support group.

The information which VOCAL provided was helpful but frightening. I also spent hours at the university library researching the subject of false sexual abuse charges. It didn't look good for us.

On the spur of the moment one day I called the kids, but Flora answered.

"Hi, Flora. Tell the kids we love them and we'll see them as soon as we can." I hung up before she could reply.

That day I also called 1-800-25-ABUSE and explained our situation. I found an empathetic ear on the other end. The woman stated that calls like mine were not uncommon, that, "some parents will take whatever means necessary to get their kids."

In the weeks that followed, I made various calls to hotline numbers and agencies. I wrote a couple of letters on behalf of the kids again to try and reach someone.

On several occasions, I contacted the prosecutor's office attempting to find out when the grand jury hearing would take place. But they were backlogged and met only on every other Thursday. That's all we knew. We had no choice but to sit and wait.

Then I wrote an editorial opinion letter entitled "Protecting the Innocent." But I never submitted it to our newspaper. Another bothersome issue that troubled Gerald and I prompted me to write this letter to the Indiana General Assembly legislators. I read through the letter one last time:

Although my husband and I are concerned citizens, parents, in my case step-parent, and health care workers, right now we sit on the other side of the fence of some very vindictive, false sexual abuse claims that, by the way, were only filed long after my husband had begun a family court case to ensure his right to see his kids. The main problem we see with the plan of broadening the criteria to include cases in which charges were merely filed, is this: Background checks on those merely accused of molestation, not charged yet, creates a law that right from the start does away with the concept of 'innocent until proven guilty.' As citizens, we work hard and believe in America and want to believe in and trust our legal system as well. If reliable sources are checked and the necessary homework on the subject of false charges is completed, an abundance of literature can be found which indicates that the latest, easiest way to obtain ownership of kids is to scream abuse. According to a legal scholar by the name of Douglas Besharov, "the charge of sex abuse is the atomic-bomb of child custody fights." (Cramer, Jerome. 1991, March 4. "Why Children Lie in Court". Time, p.76.) It stands to reason that if child abuse is claimed, it should be done before someone files for custody or visitation, not after the fact. Although, in our case, allegations were made prior to filing for visitation, a police report was not filed until shortly after a long awaited family court decision proposed to protect my husband's rights to see his sons. All we are saying is that to include a name on a registry, in cases of custody or visitation battles, before it's proven that the claims are true, and not merely a weapon which is sometimes the case, is assuming guilt and branding innocent individuals.

Please take our concerns into consideration so that perhaps many future falsely accused, truly innocent parents, mothers or fathers, will not be subjected to an unnecessary nightmare. Sadly, we realize that often when sex abuse is reported by a victim, the abuse is real, and certainly we support the prosecution of those guilty of this crime. However, we believe the justice system will continue to fail the innocent if the falsely accused are sacrificed in the process.

I also sent a letter explaining the situation to the children's outpatient psychiatrist in hopes that she would proceed with caution and help Todd and Gerry get the proper help.

Over the telephone I spoke with numerous lawyers. Then one day I visited a charismatic type, one who handles mostly men's rights in divorce cases. He offered a great deal of important advice. He emphasized the need and Gerald's right to continue to press the visitation fight while all of the side tracking was going on because as he said, "Nothing has been proven, only alleged. Somewhere down the line the court must recognize the innocent until proven guilty concept." He told us to hang in there and of course that's what we tried to do.

It's funny how in the midst of a crisis, life went on. We set the garbage cans out every Tuesday morning. On Saturdays I did the grocery shopping. The work week always felt long, but somehow we managed to struggle through it. Sporadic visits to our family and friends continued. Those friendly welcomes and an occasional night out for dinner and a movie helped to relieve the stress of all the chaos and waiting.

Then August came again. At this time last year we were having a good time at the amusement park with Todd and Gerry. This year we impatiently waited for the 23rd day of the month so we could finally convince someone that we had the right to be a family and enjoy time together this summer too.

To our surprise, the judge was in. We hoped for the best. But to our disappointment, the judge took a cautious, conservative approach and offered no further visitation until other professionals could determine if Gerald should have access to the boys, since now sexual abuse claims had been filed.

Although we were grateful for the judge's decision to appoint an impartial psychologist to evaluate the case, we felt he could have done more to review the chronological order of events. Right then and there would have been a grand opportunity for him to say, "Look, when this whole thing started, your responses to the motion for visitation modification did not mention anything about sexual abuse. Why now? And nothing has been proven. I have to proceed with an assumption of innocence until the court proves otherwise."

Instead, the judge decided to error on the side of caution. Obviously Gerald would have to prove his innocence before being granted the right to see his kids again.

That was part of the problem too. We could not see the kids. Let those boys close to their father and it may have helped to extinguish all rumors early on. Of course, observing the love between father and sons would not necessarily disprove the allegations. However, an observation of the accused with his alleged "victims" might have been enough to convince someone to look into our side of the story.

I viewed life as unfair for a long time. Somehow in this world, I kept thinking, justice's equilibrium has become horribly unbalanced when the falsely accused are persecuted while true villains are set free to hurt again and truly abused children are ignored.

Sad stories in the news also affected my spirit. Either children were being murdered by criminals set free to maim and kill again or entire towns were being disrupted and innocent lives destroyed by false charges of sexual abuse.

One day I became obsessed with the idea that if I should die suddenly for some reason, Gerald would be forced to face this absurdity alone. His main witness to what never happened and all of the good which really did occur as we cared for the boys, would never be told.

So I wrote another letter, the kind to be opened in the event of my death. The letter explained how the kids adored Ger and reiterated what a good father he was to Todd and Gerry. Especially I emphasized that I lived in the house too and never witnessed or saw any signs whatsoever indicating abuse. And if I am such a biased party, I explained, then ask our neighbors, our friends, our family. Ask the boys. After all, their statements to the police were not very credible, because they did not ring true. As usual, I included some family photos.

I began to miss the kids terribly, especially since I realized that it would probably be a long time before we could get them back.

CHAPTER 5

In autumn we began to see the court-appointed psychologist. Luckily Dr. Cobers appeared to be someone genuinely interested in helping the kids and discovering the facts. Her soft-spoken, unbiased approach made us feel at ease from the beginning.

"What I will be trying to do, Mr. and Mrs. Karlin, is collect as much information as I can from interviews with you both, with Mrs. Santeros and then with the boys, Todd and Gerry are their names, is that correct?" she asked.

"Yes," Ger confirmed.

As we sat on the comfortable couch directly across from Dr. Cobers, I felt so anxious. We had waited so long. I wanted to ramble off everything about our whole case all in one long session. But I knew it would all have to be relayed to her in fragments, over a period of time, several weeks, maybe even months.

As any good detective, reporter or psychologist would, she started at the beginning, with Gerald and Flora's divorce.

"What can I say? I met Flora and right away we were going to have a child, so we got married. But deep down, I knew it was a mistake. For awhile, I tried, really tried. Especially after she had the boys. I remember holding little Gerry in my arms and thinking nothing else mattered. I loved those little guys. But the marriage just wasn't working and I figured kids or not, what was the point in staying together if we were miserable?"

Gerald talked while Dr. Cobers jotted down notes.

"Believe me, I'm not saying that I'm perfect and I admit that I certainly have my faults and weaknesses. And I accept responsibility for my drinking and the way it was." Then Gerald jumped in to his own defense. "But Dr. Cobers, you just have to believe me. I tried to be a good father to my boys and this sex abuse stuff just never happened. To say I hurt the boys like that, it's just sick. There is no other way to describe her claims."

It was true. Neither of us were perfect as parents or anything else, but we did our best and Todd and Gerry seemed very happy with us. Things were always moving forward and getting better. I reflected as Gerald professed his innocence to the psychologist regarding the sexual abuse issue.

Dr. Cobers explained that she would be holding separate sessions with Gerald and I in order to inquire about specific issues and that his position on the claims were understood. "But for now I'd like you both to share with me a little bit about your life with the boys."

Of course I attempted to inundate her with every sweet memory that our family ever shared together. But she had a nice way of redirecting whenever it was necessary. It reminded me to slow down and let Ger talk too.

It felt great to have somebody finally listen to us.

During subsequent encounters with Dr. Cobers, Gerald and I let it all out, the sequence of events, our pain, resentment, the way we have tried to deal with the stress.

At one point we mentioned how cut off we always felt regarding medical intervention for the kids. But she stated that Gerald actually had equal rights as far as some health care issues and access to medical records.

We couldn't even get anybody to acknowledge us on the phone without the mother's signed consent. So we never dreamed that we could call up and request medical records and obtain them after presenting a written request by Gerald.

In fact, time and time again I was told that without the mother's signed consent Ger did not have access since she was the custodial parent. Once I knew the law, however, after a medical records clerk refused to help one day, I asked to speak to a supervisor at the mental health clinic where the boys were receiving counseling.

Sure enough, Dr. Cobers was right, a green light existed. Gerald and I both think of that day as a turning point. Finally we could begin to gather information and see what we were actually dealing with.

One thing especially kept bothering us. Why were the kids fine on Father's Day only to end up so traumatized a few days later and wind up in the hospital? So the first records we sought were for Todd and Gerry's hospital stay following Father's Day at our house.

What we saw literally made us sick to our stomachs. The medical records were even worse than we could have imagined. As we sat on the sofa in the boys' room, we both cried for ourselves and for the boys. We knew it was nothing but fabrication, sick lies and none of it had any factual or substantiated basis. We simply could not believe the distortions about our life together with the boys. We began to realize the damage done to the boys, yet knew there was no quick, sure way to stop it all.

Gerald looked so hurt. "You have no idea how this makes me feel." After a long silence, he blurted out, "You realize what they're saying here Karrol, that I screwed my own kids." We both sat very still, in shock, in quiet tears.

Then we decided to call the lawyer's office. That's when we found out another disturbing fact of life. There was no immediate recourse against the unsubstantiated false claims or other alluded to misrepresentations. There was no recourse. The accuser was protected by law. Confidentiality existed between client and hospital staff. We didn't sleep too well. The next morning I started in again, but Gerald stopped me short.

"Look, not today, okay. Please, let's just forget about it for a few days, all right, because to be honest, I just don't want to think about it." I understood, but knew we would have to sit down and study the records at some point in order to find a way to adequately dispute them.

Gerald left for work but I had other plans. The concept of securing some type of counseling support had been on my mind from the beginning. We never seemed to find time to make the long drive to the VOCAL support group. So I decided to arrange something local. After I got the insurance coverage straightened out, I scheduled several appointments for Ger and myself. It was a way to deal with our present emotional turmoil while at the same time would serve as a preventive measure for any impending future crisis episodes.

Although the more we spoke with Dr. Cobers, it seemed that she was always the best one to turn to. But to my dismay, she let me know that after the evaluation, a conflict of interest would mean we would not be able to rely on her anymore for support.

When the time comes to part, I'll miss her. She is such a pleasant, supportive person and a very good listener. Most importantly, she took the case, and offered to help. She didn't have to.

I decided to appeal to C.P.S. one more time for help, so I wrote again to Mrs. Arland:

> Our kids are being swept away into this mess which continues to escalate and get further from the truth, closer to a point of no return for them. If it comes down to the custody/visitation issue it's really secondary. The main thing is that Todd and Gerry have the right and need to know the truth, that their father never hurt them and that indeed he loves them and wants them in his life. We are very concerned for their emotional health and well-being at this time.
>
> Todd and Gerry's room waits for them here at their second home which they have a right to and it is filled with love, not abuse. Ask our family, our friends, neighbors. Come and visit. You would be very surprised that the bright picture you see is very different from the dark picture which was painted for you and all of the other health care workers out there.

I received no response — none whatsoever.

"C'mon, Karrol, we'll be late. We only have twenty-five minutes to get there and you know it will take a good half hour," Gerald said as he urged me to hurry.

"I already called and let Dr. Cobers know we might be just a little late. I'm ready. Let's go."

Gerald spoke first to Dr. Cobers about when he began to see the kids again. "I was going to AA and seeing this one woman, but she didn't like picking up the kids and that was the main reason I stopped seeing her. Then I ran into Karrol and it was great because she was always excited about seeing the boys. I told Flora I wanted to be a part of their lives and I was glad for a second chance. Holidays, birthday's weekends and Wednesdays at the Y. Everything's been great, until now."

Then Dr. Cobers reverted back to the alcoholism issue. "It seems as if much of your vulnerability for all of this stems from your history with alcoholism."

"Well, that sure seems to be true but it shouldn't be the issue. Look I have never denied the fact that I am a recovering alcoholic. But I am certainly not going to admit to all of the bizarre false accusations. Besides, ask Karrol, if I was drinking, I rarely went around the boys."

"It's true, Dr. Cobers," I confirmed. "Ger and I both raised those kids on a part-time basis. It wasn't as if he was home alone and drunk with the boys. I have never seen him drunk around them. And there are only a few times when he was drinking while we had them. Like one Halloween, remember Ger, I took the kids trick or treating and when I came back you had gone out and got a six-pack, so I made you take them home. And I do remember a couple times when he stopped off after work to drink some, then picked up the boys as planned and brought them home. Ger seemed fine and it was on nights when the kids had games at the 'Y', so I wasn't going to say no, take them back home and make them miss their game." I took a deep breath.

"So you're saying you were home for the most part whenever the boys came over for their visits? It was not a matter of Gerry being alone with them and drinking?" Dr. Cobers asked.

"Yes. Yet nobody pays attention to the fact that I existed, that Ger had a wife all this time or the possibility of a healthy home life. Listen, Dr. Cobers, I have a tape, I'll bring it for you if you want. It's called 'A Secret About Dad.' It was a project for a course I was taking. The boys and I are on tape and I'm explaining their dad's disease to them and how if he's sick we just can't pick them up and bring them over for their visits, but it doesn't mean that their dad doesn't love them.

I told them that since it has happened a few times and may happen once in a while, hopefully not, but if it does, to remember that we love them and we will see them as soon as their dad gets better. I made the tape because, like I said, there were a few times when Ger was supposed to get the kids and he didn't follow through. The kids would call and wonder where he was. I decided it was time to tell Todd and Gerry the truth. And do you know what the kids told me on the tape? That they knew what drunk was because of their big brother and their step-dad, the way they acted. I don't think they even ever saw Gerald that way, not during our time together anyway."

I knew that the alcoholism would be viewed as a major strike against Gerald and his character, but it was a key issue which couldn't be ignored.

"So I agree with you about his vulnerability, Dr. Cobers, but the alcoholism did not play the role that it is always alluded to as playing. So do you want to hear the tape?" I hoped for a yes.

"Sure, I'll listen to it, anything you can give me to help sort this thing out," Dr. Cobers answered.

I felt so relieved and accepted. Finally someone was listening to some of the facts and willing to study the evidence.

CHAPTER 6

"Oh great, honey," I said. "Look at this. We got our hearing date, just in time for the holidays." I handed Gerald the envelope from the prosecutor's office.

As Gerald read the date to me, we realized that both holidays, Thanksgiving and Christmas, would be affected by the madness. He took another quick look at the paperwork, mumbled a few words, and tossed it aside.

When he got busy in the other room, I picked it up and read what it said. The hearing date read December 2, 1993 at 11:30 A.M. for the molestation of Todd and Gerry, which occurred on July 15, 1993 and is being investigated.

We had always wondered where and when the alleged abuse supposedly happened. I thought, well that's impossible. It makes it sound like July 15th is an alleged date of abuse. We never saw the kids after Father's Day. In fact, that's the day the policeman called, I think.

"Well this date's stupid," I yelled to Gerald. "I'm calling the deputy prosecutor. I want to know what the heck they're talking about. Isn't that what it sounds like, honey, that July 15th is the time that it occurred?"

"Yeah, that's what it sounds like. Now who are you calling?" he asked as he came back into the living room and sat down.

"This guy here, this deputy prosecutor. It's his name all over everything." I showed him the letter again.

He looked it over again then handed it back. "Well, I doubt if you'll get anything out of him, but go ahead, call if you want. I know I can't stop you."

"I will." I dialed and got through to him right away, which surprised me.

"Well, who is this, first? Who are you?" the deputy prosecutor demanded to know after I inquired about the confusing date.

"I'm Gerald's wife, Karrol Karlin, the stepmother. I know you won't tell me anything, but..."

He cut me off. "I'm not gonna talk to YOU!" He made it perfectly clear that although he had never met me, I was guilty of something.

"Well," I persisted, "will you answer the question for my husband, about the date?"

He snapped back with another negative response. I tried one more time. "Our lawyer then?" But I heard nothing but silence on the other end. "Okay, then good-bye."

I let Gerald know what a big 'help' the guy was and how insulting the tone of his voice sounded.

"Oh, Karrol, I don't know why you keep trying the way you do. I'm sorry they keep trying to knock us down. That's what the lawyer said, that they just keep attacking until people are financially or emotionally drained, to the point when they just give up."

I said something dumb in reference to trying to be like the good guys in the movies, the way they always manage to get back up again and never die. Gerald called me a nut, told me to find something to do besides worry about the hearing. Then he kissed me on the cheek and went into the kitchen and opened the back door so he could smoke a cigarette.

An old rerun of Bonanza managed to take my mind off of things for a little while. But later that night as Gerald slept, I wrote several letters. I sent them out the next day, via certified mail.

The first one, of course, went to the deputy prosecutor I had spoken to, the others to psychiatrists, doctors, case workers, and nurses involved with the kids. I felt like it was a chance I had to take. Maybe I could reach someone. The next day at work, I decided to call a lawyer anonymously and asked him about the date, if it referred to the date of alleged abuse.

He too sounded disgusted. "I'm not answering that question over the phone! That's a felony!" As if I didn't know that Gerald could spend years rotting in jail for something he never did.

I could rarely get through to our lawyer. She was always busy with a client, so I had to rely on alternative resources which were more accessible.

The police came to mind. An officer I spoke to assumed, as we did, that the letter appeared to indicate an alleged incident of abuse on that date.

We remained anxious to discuss the plan of action regarding the hearing and obtain some more information about the dates and time periods of alleged abuse, so Gerald made an appointment with the family lawyer. It was hard to swallow, another cancellation, but it took an extra day before Gerald could see her.

He was in very poor spirits after returning home. Evidently, he felt abandoned.

"She says she can't represent me for the criminal charges since she's a family lawyer. I didn't even ask her about the date or other dates, or any other questions you gave me. Honest, Karrol, there was no point in bothering." He lifted his blue sweater over his head and walked toward the bedroom. A minute later he returned wearing his red flannel shirt.

As Gerald sat across from me, I noticed how tired and disappointed he looked. "Go ahead, hon, you can smoke in here, one cigarette. I'm okay."

"So I guess we have to hire a criminal lawyer now. I don't know, Karrol, I'm just so disillusioned about it all. I mean, I walked in there and that was it, she couldn't represent me. There wasn't much else to say. Hell, she could have told me that over the telephone."

"Yeah, really," I agreed. "Well, we'll figure it out tomorrow, okay? We have the rest of the day. Let's try and make the best of it. Hey, do you wanna go out to Freeland, make a stop at the bookstore?" I asked enthusiastically, trying to cheer him up.

Still monotone and preoccupied with his thoughts, he said, "I guess we could do that. Just let me recoup here for a little bit, all right. Then we'll go."

"Sure. Take your time."

A few days later, we hired a criminal lawyer. We had spoken to Evan Dillon a few times before regarding the allegations, since he worked in the same office as Kathleen, the family lawyer. She had even mentioned to Gerald at the last appointment that possibly Evan would take his case.

We didn't think he would settle for less than the fifteen hundred dollars up front that he had once quoted. But on November 30th, via phone, after a five hundred dollar agreed down payment arrangement and a thousand dollar balance due in two months, he agreed. "Okay, I'm in."

Both lawyers expressed concerns about us walking into the hearing professing Gerald's innocence without legal counsel present. We were very concerned too. There was no reason to trust that they would listen to us or believe a word we said.

As Mr. Dillon explained it one day in a phone conversation, "I'm telling you that if you guys walk in there screaming about your innocence and representing yourself, your gonna get screwed. Don't you get it? It's not what you say, it's all how it's presented. Even then, anything you say can and will be used against you."

He caught me off guard with such an unjust view of the way things really work. "Well, I thought we got to tell our side of the story at this point, that a jury is supposed to listen to both sides and decide. If they hear..."

But he had more bad news. "Yeah, there's a jury, a jury led by the prosecutor!"

"This is pathetic." I was angry yet laughing at the calamity of the situation. "So now like you say, we have to walk in there and play a game and plead the Fifth Amendment every time they ask something?"

"Yeah, you got it. You don't say a word and plead the Fifth." He emphasized the point again.

After I hung up I really got irritated thinking about it. I thought about the way the policeman had explained how the hearing works. It sounded like a fair opportunity to let unbiased jurors hear our side of the story. Now, I didn't know what to think.

When Gerald heard all of this he wanted to handle the situation by walking in and simply telling the truth. "I'm just going to walk in there, tell them the truth, and that's it. I don't have anything to hide. If they indict me or find me guilty at some point, then our justice system has failed us. That's all there is to it." He was dead serious.

We both wished it could be that simple. However, after speaking more with the lawyer as well as paying attention to our instincts, we decided to proceed cautiously. If an ounce of prevention could save us the grief of a pound or more of complicated trouble later, we certainly wanted to utilize it.

One night I jumped in the car and headed for my appointment with the counselor. As I waited in his office, I noticed the Big Bird and Ernie posters plastered all over the walls and the colored blocks on the floor in the corner. Obviously he works a lot with children, I thought to myself, along with a number of other things which were popping into my head. I couldn't make up my mind where to start.

When Vincint walked in, he sat directly across from me on a folding chair. I wondered about the television version of a client/shrink arrangement, a couch and a large desk. We made good eye contact as the therapy session got under way.

At one point, after much explaining and handing him a manila folder full of papers mapping out the chronological order of events, I asked him, "So do you believe me, that these claims are false?"

He answered diplomatically. "It's not really my job to say yes or no. I'm here more for the support, Mrs. Karlin, for the purpose of helping you resolve any issues you're dealing with." He waited for my reaction.

"I understand. But it's nice to know if you're talking to somebody and telling the truth, that they believe you. Nobody will listen, I thought it's your job to listen. For instance, how I was there, in the home, the abuse did not happen and there was no opportunity for it, not to mention that these claims are malicious, filed with the police after we finally get visitation back, after eight long months of trying to get our kids back into our lives. She does this and nobody will listen to us, our side." I paused for a second, then quickly added. All right, all right, here, let me ask you these two questions. Isn't it strange if a mother alleges abuse but keeps sending her kids back to the person she says is abusing her kids in a terrible way? And, do you believe that sometimes people make false charges?" I waited now, for his honest answer.

"Yes, I'll concede to a yes on both of your questions."

"Okay." I was happy with that and we moved on. In fact, I thought his answers showed integrity. How could someone listen to a half hour of one side of a story and draw solid conclusions? I told him I would have to hear the other side of the story too, before feeling like I really knew what was going on, but I was glad he saw my point on the two questions.

It felt very good to talk to somebody about the pain, frustration and stress, the constant stress.

When I walked out to the car that night, it was cold and dark. I felt some relief though and knew a good night's sleep was in store for me. The music of Kenny Loggins soothed my restlessness even more on the ride home.

The following week, it was Gerald's turn to see the counselor. I made him take the photos of our happy life together with the boys. Not that a picture is a visual graphic piece of truth, but at least he could be shown rather than just told what the boys looked like or what the four of us looked like together as a family.

In my next appointment with Dr. Cobers, we discussed the revolting medical records. I asked her questions and she asked me to discuss more elements of my life with Gerald and the boys. I mentioned other accusations in the records which I knew to be unsubstantiated and false too and offered to send along some materials to refute certain claims. It was so sickening and wrong, anyone could obviously say anything about anybody and in medical records, it shows up looking like history. The word 'allegedly' did show up often but it didn't matter. The accuser/the reporter of any fabricated tidbits of information or lies was really in control.

Then I remembered that Mr. Dillon had asked me to relay a message. "Mr. Dillon wanted me to ask you if you have anything yet and said to give him a call," I explained, acting as liaison to lawyer and psychologist.

"Well as a matter of fact, I do have a couple of thoughts from the initial interviews with the kids that maybe he should know about. Have him give me a call." She sounded so encouraging. Already, I thought. Everything else seemed to take so long.

"Well, when is a good time to reach you? He should be there right now." I put in a plug for urgency in the matter, since I knew both of them were busy people and might keep missing each other. She said she'd try.

On the evening of November 30, 1993, we met Evan Dillon for the first time in person. His office was located in the downtown area of Bradford, Indiana. I sat there wondering what he might look like because we had only spoken over the phone. When he came through the door his blond hair and the fact that he was thin surprised me. I had pictured him as heavier with dark hair.

As he quickly escorted us down the hallway to his office, Dillon came across even more of a type 'A' personality in person, almost comically at times. Abruptly he switched from one task to another. While talking to us, he dialed the phone several times, rearranged papers, stood up and sat back down, and spun around in his chair. He began talking about one issue, then darted off into a different direction, only to backtrack and finish his first point.

This went on for a good half hour. My husband and I almost got dizzy at times, but we didn't care as long as he paid attention to us well enough to answer our questions and proved to be a good lawyer.

We spoke about the date on the letter and acknowledged that it must have been some type of error since we hadn't seen the kids after Father's Day. Suddenly it occurred to me that maybe the date referred to the day the accusations were filed. But that's not what everyone seems to think.

"See, that's it right there." Dillon smiled. "They're screwed already. This whole thing is bogus and I think pretty soon they're going to realize that this case is a bunch of B.S. You know, they're gonna see that, sooner or later."

Gerald and I glanced at each other. "It sounds good to us, the sooner the better," Gerald remarked.

Then Mr. Dillon relayed some exceptional news. "By the way, I spoke with Dr. Cobers and she doesn't think you did it. The boys are dying to see you and that's just not the way it works. Usually, they don't want anything to do with the person if something happened. But they're dying to see you." He fidgeted backwards in his chair.

It was the best news anyone could have delivered to a father. "Really, she said that?"

"Oh yeah!" Dillon exulted. "But I've got to get her to come forward and say it. She's not ready because she wants to complete her evaluation. But I've got to get her to commit!" He slammed his open-faced hand down on his desktop. He amazed me by his overt style of expressing himself. "Now I understand you're up for this hearing in two days?"

"Well, you know," Gerald said, "we were thinking, as many postponements as we've had, can't you get them to postpone this thing or something until her report is done?" Ger hinted and hoped. But we both thought it was probably far too late to do something like that.

But Dillon answered back with a positive response. "That's what I've been trying to do, but I can't get a hold of the prosecutor. I keep getting a damn message." He swiveled his chair around and dialed again. No luck.

"So the kids are dying to see me, huh?" Gerald remained stuck on the good news. We smiled at each other while Mr. Dillon nodded. I reached over and took Gerald's hand and squeezed.

We left the office that night with a tentative plan of action. Since our appointment had gone well and we felt like we had accomplished something, we decided to take advantage of our uplifted spirits and stopped on the way home at a quaint neighborhood restaurant.

A flashing light on the message machine, after we got home, let us know someone had called. The happy mood of the evening continued. "Yes, Evan Dillon here. I'm calling for Gerald. Yes, uh, Gerald, listen, I just talked to the prosecutor and told him you weren't going to testify. So you don't have to go Thursday. So just forget about it. Go to work, whatever.

They are not going to indict you on Thursday. Thursday's absolutely out. It looks like they're going to wait on Dr. Cobers' report. So, I'll see you or talk to you guys later. Okay. Good-bye."

Gerald and I exchanged a couple of high fives, then hugged and kissed. We simultaneously felt the winds changing course. We knew we weren't out of the woods yet, but the positive results of the evening felt like a major turning point for us and the kids. It was the closest thing to achieving anything in our favor since the whole thing had begun.

If we can just get them to wait on Dr. Cobers' report, we kept thinking, hopefully that will resolve everything in our favor. Then we could relax, and see the kids again.

CHAPTER 7

The Grand Jury hearing was rescheduled for December 2nd. Gerald and I awoke early to prepare ourselves, but at 8:30 A.M. the phone rang and we received some good news, another last minute postponement. We felt some relief, yet realized that it would be awhile longer until the situation could be resolved.

"I think somebody is starting to listen and see the truth, maybe the pictures I sent helped. No, I know what it is," I said to Gerald. "It's that deputy prosecutor attorney. Maybe he really does have a conscience."

Ger smiled and rolled his eyes. "I'm just glad we don't have to go through all that today. Now I don't want to talk about it anymore for the day, okay? Let's take a break, all right?" he pleaded. It was a request he made often.

That evening Gerald and I got all dressed up and attended the Hoosier Word-Hunter's Christmas party. Many of my poetry club friends were there accepting awards. I received an honorable mention for a poem entitled "Nature's Treasure."

Prior to receiving word about the hearing cancellation, I was skeptical about going to the annual event, since I didn't think we would be able to enjoy ourselves. Surrounded and inspired by a room full of writers and poets, Ger and I managed to live for the moment that night. We were so happy to be there, temporarily free of worries. The stimulating, positive, friendly environment made for an exceptional evening. It was the kind of night out that we needed to balance out our daily chaotic, troubled existence.

The following week, Dr. Cobers continued her evaluation of Gerald. She recommended an appointment with a drug and alcohol therapist. We did not really have the two hundred and thirty-five dollars to spare, but we wanted to comply, to follow through with anything which might help.

So he scheduled the appointment. The results confirmed what Gerald and I already knew. "Yep, I've got a history, I'm a recovering alcoholic." After I reminded him about the fact that he had been lax about attending AA meetings and that it might be a good idea to prove that we are both willing to do whatever it takes to continue to provide a healthy, alcohol-free household for the kids, he became less flippant with his remarks.

A few days later, I mailed out another weekly payment to Dr. Cobers inside a Christmas card. I wrote a note to the effect that Gerald had contacted his sponsor again and stated that he would reconnect to some degree with AA and/or an addiction counselor.

I emphasized again that Flora had managed to displace the real focus. We hadn't encountered any trouble related to the kids and Gerald's alcoholism for a long time. The question concerns Flora's sexual abuse allegations, I reiterated, not the issue regarding Gerald's history of alcoholism. And as a matter of fairness, we could not refrain from pointing out that, "If professionals sincerely watching out for Todd and Gerry's best interests want to assure that the kids remain in an alcohol-free home, it might prove helpful to investigate their living situation with their mother, since we had heard many stories from the kids regarding their step-father's frequent drinking habits.

I thought about the whole situation one day, especially the fact that the alcoholism had made Gerald so vulnerable. Certainly, we could not deny that specific ghost or skeleton that was or is part of our existence. But I wished that people could see Gerald as a loving father, a caring, sincere parent who provided a long-term quality part-time home and lifestyle for the kids. That was the Gerald I knew, fighting back. Certainly human beings or parents are much more than their pasts or diseases or weaknesses, especially when people stand firm and fight back in a healthy way. Why couldn't they see that, I wondered.

As the rescheduled grand jury hearing seemed imminent, it became difficult again to keep focused on important matters. A sporadic, obsessive-compulsive behavioral pattern resurfaced and, quite frankly, got on my nerves. I called it the FASA syndrome, which stood for Falsely Accused of Sexual Abuse. I always included myself as accused, although it was Gerald who was actually named because I had lived in the house too during the time period of alleged abuse.

To fondly remember those years with the boys and have someone paint a false ugly picture, the pain and frustration was almost unbearable at times.

Something else began to plague me at the crossroads we had reached, the 'limbo' mode. In other words, it was the waiting, not knowing which created an aching restlessness and disharmony. We had no choice but to impatiently wait. We could only hope that it would all end soon.

One night we laid next to each other in bed while David Letterman cracked jokes and Tiger snored near the doorway. I looked through a People Magazine while Gerald began to read the final chapter of his magical adventure book. There were about ten books in the series and he had read every one of them.

"I mean, really, Karrol, we can go on and on about this, say what we think, what we know, but the bottom line is that there's people out there that are going to have their own ideas about the truth. So I don't know what to expect."

"Yes, people who only have bits and pieces of information, people who have been purposely misled," I pointed out.

"Yeah. And I can't really sway them in any direction," he lamented. "I'm really just going to be at their mercy."

"You're right," I agreed. "You can't do much but answer questions at this point. It's not fair, none of this is fair. But none of this will be in vain either, sweetheart. Trust me on that one, okay?"

He managed a smile and started to read again.

I remembered something else he once told me. He made me promise that if anything ever happened to him, that I would make sure I cleared this thing up for him. He didn't want Todd and Gerry to go through life believing he ever did those awful things or didn't love them.

As he wished, I swore to him that I'd never give up. I yawned, thought about my promise and pulled the covers over my head. Winter's mean spirit had fallen upon us for the last few weeks and it was freezing outside.

Life continued, but not without problems. Gerald went deaf in one ear until a doctor cured him by removing a long slender piece of wax. One car conked out, then the other one due to the bitter cold. With a new set of spark plugs, at least we managed to get one car going. We wondered what else could go wrong.

For five years I had worked at Lucy's, as her private duty nurse, but unfortunately, her insurance ran out, which meant I was out of a job. I worried about what she and I both would do. Just what Ger and I needed, I thought, more financial stress. It was very bad timing.

Yet, believe it or not, I knew that things could be worse. As much as I hated to be dealing with a crisis, as I watched the horror stories on the news about the devastating California earthquake, the thought of simply having a roof over our heads was a blessing.

Finally the subpoena came. We received one in the mail and one inside the screen door on January 5, 1994. This time there were two different addresses under Gerald's name, and two different times they required him to be present. The claims had become even more ambiguous. The July 15th date now read, "molestations which occurred in Echo County."

Around this time, after the usual delays and confusion, I also got a hold of the June 30th police report which Flora had filed. Again, the alleged date of abuse written on the report didn't make any sense. The date showed November 14, 1992 and said "approximately."

It hit me right away. That happened to be the date that Gerald filed for modification of visitation rights. I checked our calendars. The only day we did have the boys around that time was on November 7th and Gerald was at work, while I picked up the kids for a two-hour visit. If memory serves me correctly, we went to the arcade at the mall for a little bit, then home for about a half hour so the boys could see their room and Tiger.

I set the paper down on the table and dialed Dr. Cobers. Luckily I reached her instead of her answering machine. "Hi Dr. Cobers, this is Karrol Karlin. How are you?" I asked.

"Okay, what's up?"

"Oh, first of all, I want to let you know we mailed a payment yesterday. But when we got home today, I found another notification that they set up another hearing for January 20th. Do you know anything about this? I knew it was coming, but we thought we'd hear from you first, that your report was done."

"No," she explained, "this is the first I'm hearing about this. Have you called Evan yet? Is he aware of this?" she asked.

"No, not yet. I wanted to call you first. I thought maybe you were done with your evaluation or something."

"Well, no, not really. I can certainly pull together some of the materials I've drawn up, but the main thing I'm still having trouble with are the records. I can't get any medical records from Dr. Tano or their new psychiatrist at the clinic." She conveyed her frustration in the matter.

"But I don't understand. Doesn't Flora just sign a consent to release them or can't the judge help you? I thought you could get the records since he recommended you."

She spoke again of her inability to obtain the records and advised me to call Evan Dillon.

So I called and left a message, since he was busy with a client. I waited by the telephone.

When he called back, I explained about the new hearing date and the fact that Dr. Cobers could not obtain the medical records she needed.

I also voiced some other concerns. "I'm so worried they're going to indict," I said. "It all seems so unfair. We have told them the truth, why do they choose to believe the lies without investigating our side of the story? And why didn't they wait on her report?" I rambled on and didn't give Mr. Dillon a chance to cut me off this time. "And listen, Evan, I want you to get us contact with Todd and Gerry's new doctor at the clinic. I don't want them to keep receiving counseling for sexual abuse by their father when it never happened. They need help with the real issues. Don't you see that they can still bounce back right now? They've done it before. Somebody's got to think about Todd and Gerry here before it's too late for them."

After my passionate speech, Mr. Dillon said he empathized with my concerns but that he had to focus on the possible criminal charges of sexual abuse, that his job is to try and to help Gerald, not the kids.

My concern was for Gerald's welfare too, but I was also worried about the kids. I just couldn't believe how the whole nightmare kept snowballing.

Finally, before he hung up, he told Gerald and I to hurry and do whatever we could to obtain the medical records.

CHAPTER 8

Gerald and I spent a full week obtaining medical records for Dr. Cobers, and sometimes it was no easy task. After educating one medical records clerk to the law, Indiana code 16-39-1-7, formerly 16-4-8-14, because someone had informed me about it, we were still refused access. The clerk explained her rationale and right to refuse. "This is a sex abuse case. We're not going to give you the records. There are exceptions, you know, and this law's not in black and white anyway. There are exceptions and we have the right to refuse."

"Well, do you have a court order that limits us access to the records, because that is the exception," I asked knowingly.

"No," she replied.

"Well, then, Gerald has a right to the records," I informed her. "Are you going to comply with the law or not?" I stopped talking and took a deep breath. "We need those records for Dr. Cobers, who is the court-appointed psychologist. She's in the midst of an evaluation for Todd and Gerry's case, and she asked us to obtain them for her. All I want to know today is what my husband has to do to come and get them."

She was not convinced. "Well, I'm sorry, but we can't help you. It would have to be done through lawyers."

"Okay then, I'll talk to our lawyer, but in the meantime, Gerald will be dropping off a written request for those records. Thank you. Good-bye." I hung up.

I spent a few moments enduring the frustration, then got busy and made more calls. After hooking up the individuals refusing the records with the judge's secretary, who made it clear that we had every right to the documents, they conceded. Not only that, but we received a cordial, apologetic letter a few days later in the mail as well as speedy, friendly cooperation thereafter from the clinic.

Also, shortly after providing a copy of the health care equal rights statute to Dr. Tano's office and the original hospital which Todd had been admitted to, Dr. Cobers quickly received an influx of medical records.

People began to treat Gerald as a human being who had rights too. Yet, until he was given an opportunity to refute the accusations made against him, or until Todd and Gerry came forward with the truth, I knew Gerald would be considered guilty of the alleged horrible crimes against his own sons.

It helped tremendously to know that many people around us, especially family members and Dr. Cobers believed in us. There were a couple of loose ends to tie up, so Gerald and I provided more information regarding the false allegations in an at attempt to dispel any doubts whatsoever. We pointed out discrepancies and various inconsistencies regarding Flora and the boys' stories. We handed over a list of dates taken from our calendars which indicated all of the kids' visits. And we kept emphasizing to Dr. Cobers that there was no physical evidence and that the boys denied the accusations for so long. Yet, now their tales seemed to be growing with every new doctor or therapist they came in contact with.

Sadly, from the most recent records, it seemed that Todd and Gerry were adapting to a false, painful reality. They had too. It was a matter of survival. The psychologist explained that many long hours were spent by the fireplace reading over the materials of our case. She kept referring to the timing of things, which seemed critical to pointing out certain facts and things which didn't make sense, like Flora returning the boys to Gerald so often after accusing him so early on.

During one session, she came up with a great idea, a poster board to show the chronological order of events. I couldn't wait to be sitting in the court room. She'd pull out the enormous, impressive visual aid for the jurors to see which would provide clincher clues for Gerald's defense and prove the accused did not do it. Then everyone would see with clarity what a reckless travesty it had all been. Especially the judge, who would immediately grant us an overdue reunion with Todd and Gerry. I couldn't wait. Visitation would be a start. I began to feel better about our prospects of being a family again.

Ger and I worried constantly about the kids. Often we would sit and look at our photo albums and remember the good old days. Whether it was a picture of the boys jumping on the trampoline, or constructing a snowman in the front yard or a snapshot of Todd carrying a bag of trash out, the reflections served to help us momentarily feel close again.

"Precious memories," I said to Ger, "at least nobody can take those away from us." And yet as I read more and more about cases like ours, especially when children are kept away from one parent for so long, I began to harbor a secret fear. I worried about the very real possibility that somehow Todd and little Gerry's memories would be damaged and the prospect that the special times they had spent with their dad might be lost, somehow, forever.

Gerald endured the crisis day by day. I recall one night, I had rented a video about a kidnapped boy who reunites with his natural family. Tears were unusual for Gerald. I apologized for renting it. He shrugged his feelings off and told me to play the next movie. Luckily it was a comedy.

The January hearing came and went. It was simple. We were advised not to go by our criminal lawyer, Dillon, so we didn't. He simply told us it would probably be a couple of months before we heard anything.

I said, "Fine, by that time, hopefully, we'll be back in court with Dr. Cobers' report, we'll have the kids back in our lives and they can hoot and holler all they want to about this lie or that one. By that time perhaps the love they witness between Todd, Gerry and their dad will force them to realize how unfair it was to keep us from being a family."

If only the daydream would come true. "That's what's so sad, they won't listen." I explained our situation to my girlfriend as she sat across from me as we dined at the Rose Garden. "I have called and written letters, but that main lady at CPS, she simply refuses to check into our side of the story. She says it's closed as far as they're concerned. It's in the prosecutor's hands now. I don't know what else to do." I shouted the last few words because three tables away, the waitresses were serenading someone on their birthday.

"So in other words," she said, "nobody will help you right now, you just have to wait until this is all resolved first? That's just not right. The kids seemed so happy with you guys. You'll get them back. It's sad, Karrol, but right now you just have to be strong and see it through, that's all you and Gerald can do." She offered her advice and words of encouragement.

We continued to carry on our conversation while we nibbled and filled up on breadsticks and salad. She drank a tasty Margarita while I savored a Tom Collins.

After dinner, she dropped me off at home, since she had to get home to her kids. I sat down in the comfortable rocking-chair and decided to make some calls. The first call went to a gentleman located in Cardinal City, someone I had contacted once before. We spoke for at least forty-five minutes. He offered more support and cleared up a few things. He was uncertain, however, if in Indiana, like some other states, private citizens were required by law to report suspected abuse.

It brought to mind a notorious case in the news. I thought about all of the parents and employees who came forth only after the allegations of sexual abuse were made. Did they break the law by not reporting if they felt that a child needed protection from a suspected abuser, I wondered? Following another call to a police officer in Los Angeles, California, I found out that in that state, only certain professionals were mandated to report suspected abuse. He rambled off the penal code for the state. I wondered about Indiana law.

Certainly, I realized the ethical responsibility of the average citizen to report suspected abuse, but it was obvious if it was against the law not to report and people feared ramifications for not doing so, then many of the belated alleged witnesses in this case, as well as in other cases, may never have come forward so late in the game.

Then I called Laura, the person who had paced the halls at the Little City court house the same day as we did. I explained how out of control our case had gotten. She couldn't believe it. I wished her and her husband good luck, since they had been victorious in their fight and his three daughters lived with them now.

"Okay, well, keep in touch and let us know how you two are doing. And hang in there," she encouraged me.

"We will. You too. Thanks a lot. See you and take care."

Suddenly I remembered that Tiger was still outside, in the back yard. I began to panic. Sure enough, he had slipped on a patch of water which had frozen over. Quickly, I carried him inside and threw a blanket around him. Luckily, he perked up and looked like he would be all right. Since added stress always makes me more careless and forgetful, I made a mental note and promise to myself to be more careful.

When Gerald came home from work, I told him about the calls I had made and the emergency with Tiger.

He kneeled down to pet him. "Did you get stuck on the ice old man, you gonna be okay, buddy?" He looked him over to make sure he was all right. "Well, thank God, you found him when you did. It's freezing out there." He pampered Tiger a little more, then went to take his uniform off.

The following morning, after starting the day out right by making love, Gerald went to work while I continued to bother people for information. I also addressed the matter of trying to find a job.

During one phone call, it was explained to me by a person supposedly knowledgeable on the subject, that unless a File 13, 310 allegation type of official report had been received by our attorney or us, that in most probability Gerald's name would not be on the child molester's registry list. The voice on the other end of the phone said, "The computer system might be ready by June, but I doubt it." I learned that it was impossible for Ger's name to be locked in some computer somewhere as an accused molester because the system wasn't ready yet.

A representative involved with the passage of Indiana Public law 142-193, confirmed the fact that the registry would include alleged molesters too, those people merely accused, not convicted yet. "But it would be up to the officer in charge, or judge involved in the case to call in the name and report it to the registry," she clarified.

After collecting some more names and addresses, I decided to write some more letters, although I was told a long time ago that it wouldn't help.

Then I ran across Mr. Buntley's telephone number, a child advocate I had spoken with several times. During our discussion, he made the point that intentions are good regarding the changes in the law, because abusers quickly move and go elsewhere, to another state or country. A national registry could help by letting people know ahead of time that a certain person has a history of child molestation.

But one day at the library, I had found an article in one of our local newspapers that told about New York and how they were having so much trouble regarding this matter. The article in the paper said that many people who are placed on the list do not belong there and that the standard of evidence used in order to place a suspect's name on the list was in question, and could possibly lead to a 'high risk of error.' In other words, a federal appeals court acknowledged the gravity of the sexual abuse problem, but it stressed that lawmakers would simply have to go back to the drawing board to perfect the good-intentioned, but flawed, inequitable reporting system.

Gerald believed that two separate lists should exist, one for convicted individuals and one for the accused. He had read somewhere about the process of removing a name from the list once a person is found innocent or the case is dropped. It sounded like another lengthy, perhaps costly appeal would be necessary. This didn't seem fair at all if a person was innocent. He was right. When an accused person is exonerated of the charges, that name should come off immediately. I felt the flaw lied in not being able to convict those truly guilty and trying to convict innocent people.

My idea was to have the accused sign an agreement to contact a certain authority if moving is planned. If this was not done as agreed and the accused moved and did not notify someone, then the opportunity to remain anonymous would be nullified. This way, an alleged abuser is protected by law until exoneration, conviction, and or relocation. In essence, the accused cooperates enough to prevent the ease with which true abusers can escape, yet he or she is treated innocent until proven guilty. But it was still a compromise and didn't seem right. I figured anyone can charge anyone with anything. And right from the start they're treated as guilty, denied privileges, etc. It didn't make any sense.

My mind kept spinning as I tried to process all of the information and ideas ruminated about all morning long.

About noon I took a break and made a ham and cheese sandwich and snacked on some pretzels. I poured an R.C. Cola into a glass along with two ice cubes. I laid down to watch some television, but the next thing I knew it was two-thirty in the afternoon. The nap was refreshing.

When I checked the mail, I noticed a packet from the Attorney General's office. I read through the interesting materials. Somewhere down the line, Ger and I knew there had to be a measure that attempted to prevent false reports and hold false reporters accountable.

In section 20.8C.31-6-11-24 of Public Law 142-1993, it states: "A person who intentionally communicates to (1) a law enforcement agency; or (2) a local child protection service; a report of child abuse or neglect knowing the report to be false commits a Class B misdemeanor." It went on to say that the false reporter is liable.

We had inquired about this several times, what are the rights we can pursue, what is our recourse? We never got a satisfactory answer. "Well, sure you can sue her," our attorneys would say, "but what are you going to achieve if she doesn't have any money?" That wasn't the point. We just wanted to know that people could not get away with falsely accusing someone, especially of something so terrible. We hoped that when the time came, the proper authorities would do their job and hold Flora accountable for all the damage she had done. That was the whole point.

Knowledge of legal recourse prompted me to make one more call to the prosecutor's office. While the female voice could not explain what a misdemeanor would entail, she inferred that I had the right to call the police and ask how I would file a report regarding the filing of a false report.

Within an hour, I stood dickering with an officer, urging him to take my report. When I finally convinced him, it felt so good, like Gerald and I had rights again. We were being considered the victims finally.

I realized the obsession with the matter was unhealthy. But I spent the whole afternoon writing even more letters to attorneys, the police, even the prosecution.

After a few days, I returned home from grocery shopping to find a message on the answering machine.

"Yes, Karrol, Gerald, Evan Dillon here. Karrol, you have been conferring with the prosecutor again. I have to warn you that you should not be corresponding with them. They want to put Gerald in jail. Don't you know you're doing more harm than good? You may have already irrevocably damaged your husband's case. I have to urge you not to write or talk to them, anymore. The photos, for instance, they can use them any way they want or any part of something you send as trying to beg for mercy. Trying to persuade them that Gerald's innocent makes him sound guilty!"

I cringed. It was a message only I needed to hear, so I erased it right away. It felt like an old-fashioned scolding. I guess I deserved it though and it made me feel rotten to think that maybe I had jeopardized Ger's case.

In retrospect, I suppose words like 'framed' should not have been used. It could, I finally realized, sound like a guilty person feigning innocence. I knew it would probably be a long time before I tried to communicate again with the opposition. Although I did toy with the idea of asking our lawyer's permission to write to the governor.

One day, frazzled as usual about the whole situation, especially the ongoing one-sided investigation, I called Dr. Cobers. "I just can't wait until this thing is over so we can go on with our lives." I hung up hoping to see her soon. I remained preoccupied with the notion that the next knock at the door could be the police demanding to handcuff Ger and drag him off to be humiliated and unjustly jailed.

Both Gerald and I began to get jumpy.

CHAPTER 9

On one of our more relaxing evenings, Gerald and I entertained each other by playing Scrabble. Tiger kept us company too as he paced in circles, bumped into walls and stood in the corner like he forgot something. Poor thing, first it was his hearing, then his eyesight. I realized his days were probably numbered.

The phone rang, but we were concentrating on our next play and didn't feel like being bothered, so we let the answering machine take the message. The volume was turned down, so after his play, Gerald retrieved the message to see if it was anything important. The minute he pushed the button, I heard our lawyer's voice. I jumped up.

"Yes, Gerald, this is Evan Dillon. I've got some bad news. I have to inform you that you were indicted today. It's two counts of a Class B Felony, that's what they're charging you with. So I had to call and tell you. As soon as you get this message give me a call back, as soon as possible." It was another day ruined.

"Why is she doing this? Why is this happening? Why, God, why?" Gerald asked as he gritted his teeth. "They won't look at this visitation thing or wait on Dr. Cobers. Why? Goddammit. This is so sick, so utterly wrong."

I began to cry and sat down on the desk chair across from him in the study. Realizing how hurt Gerald felt, I grasped for words, but there was nothing I could say to ease the pain or make it go away. After his initial expression of anger and disillusionment, he remained silent and sat very still while staring into space. It was as if the horror of the moment was frozen in time.

We knew immediately of some of the consequences. There would be more turmoil, more lost time from his work, and more injury to Gerald's dignity. Certainly we knew it would involve much more money, but most of our money was already gone.

And what about Todd and Gerry? More than ever we wanted to say to them and the world, that our times were special, our memories nothing to be ashamed of, because the abuse never happened. We were prohibited from letting Todd and Gerry know how much they were loved, missed and wanted.

I could sense the rage and disbelief boiling inside my body. I stood up and began to pace and rant and rave. "My God, Gerald, what are we supposed to do now? Are they really going to come and get you and put you in jail? I don't understand. I just don't believe this is happening." But he just sat there staring at the wall. He internalized everything. It worried me terribly.

Now we had an indictment to add to our pain. I wondered about publicity, if Gerald's name would be plastered all over the front page of our daily newspaper as a child molester.

The horrible nightmare dragged on day after day. Emotionally, it was awfully painful. Gerald and I both tried to go on about our daily business, but we felt so wounded and powerless.

Once in awhile I would dream about Todd and Gerry, see their sweet faces. From a distance, they would wave to me, then I'd awaken and they would disappear.

Financial problems became more stressful because, although I did manage to find some home health care work, in three weeks time the elderly woman I had grown fond of had to return to rehab. So my contribution was limited to a sporadic, and on-call nursing jobs, and helping out Lucy only occasionally since she had to pay on her own now.

There were glimpses of light as wintertime subsided and warmer, occasionally sunny days arrived. But mostly Gerald and I felt like we were being held captive in the dark without a way to escape.

It hurt, watching someone working so hard and trying to stay healthy and productive continually receive malicious blows to the heart, mind and soul.

"I know what they're gonna do," Ger told me one day following the indictment, "it will be that fear tactic, you know, the prosecutor will tell our lawyer, 'Look, if your client doesn't plead guilty right here and now to a lesser charge, then he's going up the river for a very long time.' "

But Gerald made it clear from the very beginning that he would not compromise. "I'm not pleading guilty to something I

68

didn't do. I don't care what they say or what they do. And I am not going to jail. Never. They just better wake up and realize the truth here."

One evening as we sat on the sofa reviewing the disturbing medical records again, Gerald became extremely discouraged. "What's the point? What's the goddamn point? What's the use of doing anything, trying to get Todd and Gerry back, going to work, thinking about becoming a paramedic? I'll just lose it all anyway when they drag me off to jail." The medical records were hard to swallow. He was feeling the hopelessness and helplessness of all of his efforts.

The moment reminded me of a movie with Harry Morgan, Walter Matthau and Stephanie Zimbalist, in which a young boy asks the very same question one day about tackling his paper route amidst a family crisis: "What's the point?" Harry Morgan tells him, "Because it helps." I knew better than to say anything though. I kept silent and let Gerald continue to say whatever he wanted.

"How can I ever look the boys in the eye again, Karrol, if they think I did this stuff to them? It looks like we've lost Todd now too, see right here on this page." He pointed to a specific segment of the latest hospital medical record. "See, he's giving up now too. They've got him believing it. He was the one trying to hang in there and stick up for me all along. Poor kid. God, I can't believe these guys have to go through this sick bull shit. I just don't want them to end up messed up from all this, you know?" He set the records down on the end table and looked at me.

I still didn't know what to say. I struggled for something optimistic. "I know it's so unfair, sweetheart, but the truth comes out. It will. You guys will work it out. It will probably take some time and counseling for a while. But someday you guys will get it back."

Somehow we managed to distance ourselves somewhat from our worries for the rest of the evening. We rented a couple of action movies from the video store. I guess we just wanted to escape for a while.

In the following days, with Gerald's new "warranted" criminal status, tensions ran high. I guess what hit hardest was the realization that our crisis was far from over. Abuse laws meant to protect children were being exploited and Gerald's freedom was in serious jeopardy.

I worried incessantly about the possibility that I had made it worse for Gerald by writing and calling people. I wondered which piece of information they might take out of context and twist around to their advantage.

Finally this conflict was alleviated to a large degree one night as I sat and watched 'Rescue 911.' I came to the conclusion that the whole situation was similar to running across someone who needs CPR. If I'm the only one on the scene, I learned a long time ago that it's important to take the risk and do whatever I can to help because if not, waiting for someone else to come around and take action might prove fatal for the innocent victim.

The concept of trying to help also brought back to mind my last year in high school, a few days before graduation. As I walked down the hallway, my English Lit teacher handed me a very special ink pen. I kept reading the inscription on it over and over because the saying was so beautiful. As time went on, I learned that the hard part of the famous prayer is, "...and the wisdom to know the difference."

If our crisis was some kind of test or something as Ger had once remarked, then it would be important to realize someday, whether it was time to keep trying or time "...to accept the things..." we could not change.

Although we were both tired of trying and getting nowhere, we weren't ready to give up fighting.

When Gerald got home that night, I reheated the pot roast I had cooked earlier. After supper I told him about the inspiring stories aired on 'Rescue 911', and 'America's Most Wanted,' one case especially about a family that was all torn apart but finally reunited after twenty years. He knew exactly what I was hinting to. I had mentioned before about similar episodes that shared stories of tearful reunions.

"Yeah, twenty years, I'll probably be dead in twenty years. I just hope the boys take it upon themselves to look up the court records someday. That they search for the truth at some point and realize how much I loved them."

The following day, Mr. Dillon called and said he needed to talk to Gerald. I let him know about what time he would be home. I only understood bits and pieces from listening to Gerald's end of the conversation, but it quickly became apparent that we had a failure to communicate with our own lawyer.

Both Evan Dillon and the family lawyer had been helpful and supportive, certainly flexible and patient as far as monetary reimbursement. But all of a sudden we had another problem. From the beginning all we wanted was our day in court, the ability to walk into family court and say, "We're here, we just want the boys back." Now, with the pending criminal charges, we simply wanted to get into court as quickly as possible, address the real issues and put it all behind us. But our lawyer's idea was to play the 'Matlock' angle, to walk in court and convince the judge or jury that someone else had committed the crime, which would, in turn, prove Gerald's innocence. Neither Ger or I thought much of this particular twisted strategic suggestion. For one thing, it only worked for Matlock because he always managed to find the real culprit.

In our case, of course, we knew there was no real culprit because the kids had not been subjected to any crime. Not the one alleged anyway. We weren't about to waste time and energy on some misdirected attempt to possibly get Gerald a lesser sentence or some handed-down decision which would leave him branded for the rest of his life. It was important to us to expose the facts and hopefully convince people of the truth, because we knew that only the truth would set the kids free, as well as Gerald.

I remembered something that I had read one day. Not guilty only proves a conviction was not achieved, whereas the word innocent represents the concept that there is no guilt on the part of the accused. So often in the cases I had read about regarding false charges, the accused remained suspect long after being found not guilty. In fact, it was not uncommon for a falsely accused victim to either have his or her life ruined. In some instances, the ordeal proved to be unbearable, and unfortunately, the victim chose suicide as the last resort resolution.

The aftershock of the actual indictment challenged us to maintain our sanity. But there was definitely some irrational thinking going on. Gerald entertained fleeting understandable notions extracted from the song "Travelin' Man" while I too envisioned us traveling south or west or somewhere toward a warmer, friendlier climate.

Admittedly the non-viable idea of suicide did enter my thoughts once in a while. But I figured if people could live through the horror of concentration camps and other ungodly nightmares, then Gerald and I could survive this.

We wondered, though, if, when and how it would ever come to an end. From Dillon, we learned that bail was set at three thousand dollars. Gerald would have to surrender, then we could bail him out. It was no time for jokes, but I couldn't help thinking that the kids always did cost us double. One child and the bond would have been cut in half.

As the situation intensified, everyone kept telling us the same thing. "We believe in you, Gerald, and we know you adore those kids and didn't do this. We'll pray for all of you."

I prayed. It didn't seem to help anymore. I would regain my positive spirit off and on and think of things like my handicapped friends, how challenging life is for them, yet they keep fighting. Or after seeing 'Rescue 911,' I'd think about all of the good people in the world. But I couldn't help it, bitterness was taking over. It got harder to enjoy anything or believe in God or the goodness of the world.

One night, while lying in bed listening to some Don Henley, I tried writing some poetry for cathartic relief. I thought, how apropos, his song, "The End of the Innocence."

Since I felt that for now we had lost Todd and Gerry, but hoped to find them again someday, I called the poem, "Lost and Found Again Someday." That was it. Our kids were waiting at the lost and found crossroads of life and we had no rights to pick them up and bring them home.

Is there a safe corner of truth
a dignified nest of comfort to crawl into
when the world gets you down?
When innocence and justice are slaughtered,
made mockery of,
and lost to "the summer winds."
'Ol Blue Eyes reminds us all
of the siren songs of jazzy peace
and our souls revel in
but refute the saddest blues
for respites from grief.
Bad, twisted deeds upon our backs.
Why not fruitful God-seeds instead?
The inquisitive cry of why and wishes.
Children, transformed
into low-life chess pieces,
with no moves of their own.
Vulnerable and trusting
in a false peril of reality.
Then swept away
in a gush of blood and tears
to a point of no return.
Unless the ripple effects of love
can still the night
and shine the light toward home.

CHAPTER 10

Arrangements were made with the prosecutor's office for Gerald's surrender. But Mr. Dillon said that it might be a good idea if we stayed somewhere else for the night, just in case the opposition decided to jump the gun. So we signed in at a low economy motel room. As I looked around, the drab room consisting of a bed, dresser, small table, television and stained carpeting instantly made me feel homesick.

Gerald called Dillon again from the motel room after we got settled. He asked him, "What's the difference in me walking in by myself or walking in with you?" Then he inquired about another idea. "Couldn't you get them to give me a little more time to try and get some money together for the bond? We're calling around, but it's going to take some time, because we just don't have it."

Apparently Dillon acknowledged that it was Gerald's prerogative if he wanted to walk in alone. He also offered to call and try to buy Gerald some time.

Fifteen minutes passed by and the phone rang again. The surrender could wait until Monday morning. Then Gerald would have to appear or they would come looking for him. But Dillon cautioned Gerald to stay put because a warrant was in effect, so if he was stopped for a traffic violation or had any contact with the law, he would be arrested right on the spot.

"We only have so much in savings, honey, I'm going to have to call Rennie and Perry and ask for their help," I emphasized while reaching for the phone.

He sighed but didn't argue. We had one choice, borrow money. Otherwise, Gerald would have to sit in jail.

We laid on the bed discussing our dilemma, making plans then changing them. One thing we decided not to go through with was contacting the press again in the morning. After speaking with the reporter, we tossed the number in the garbage. We wanted people to know that there was something terribly wrong happening. There was a chance that some agency or somebody would step in and take an impartial look, even force

CPS and health care professionals to speak with Dr. Cobers and protect the kids until we could straighten the whole mess out.

But we refrained. Instead, we decided to sit on our story and present it to those who judged Gerald so blindly and perhaps the world, when the time was right.

After a few hours of sleep, morning came like it always did. I took it upon myself to contact the charismatic lawyer over in Southparker, Illinois again. Since he was experienced in divorce issues and the false allegation aspects, he seemed like the right one to turn to. I figured Paul R. Leggan would know that the best defense was the truth. Gerald gave me the green light to talk to him but he also made it clear that he didn't want to go. He promised to stay put and wait on the important incoming calls we were expecting.

Luckily, Leggan (pronounced Lej/jun) was in on Saturday mornings. I arrived at nine with hopes of getting a chance to speak with him right away. But I would have waited all day. In my pocket, I had what I considered to be a large sum of money ready to hand over to him if he consented to be Ger's lawyer.

"Hello," I said to the receptionist, "could you please tell Mr. Leggan I need to talk to him, if possible. He is in, isn't he?"

"Yes, he's here, and your name?" she asked.

"Karrol Karlin. I spoke with him before. I know I don't have an appointment but could you tell him it's kind of an emergency?" I asked politely.

The receptionist replied, "Certainly." She went directly to his office to give him the message.

Leggan stepped out of his office and waved me in.

My heart started to race as I anticipated the task of trying to hire Mr. Leggan.

Yes, Karrol. Hi. Come on in and sit down. What can we do for you? What's going on?" He sounded curious.

"Well, Mr. Leggan, they did it, they indicted my husband yesterday. Two counts of felony charges for molestation of his own kids. You remember our case that we talked about before, the modification thing with Todd and Gerry, my stepsons, the two boys," I hurriedly explained.

"Yes, yes, I do remember. What are their ages again?"

I responded by giving him the ages of the boys when everything started and their current ages. He asked a few more formality questions and jotted down all of my answers. Then he told me to tell him what happened at the grand jury hearing.

"We never went."

"You didn't go?" He seemed surprised.

"No. Our lawyer said not to go, that we shouldn't testify. They were supposed to wait on Dr. Cobers' report, remember, the court-appointed psychologist. But they didn't." As I talked I tried to get comfortable in the chair, but I couldn't.

"Now what did I tell you I was going to do about the hearing?" He referred back to my response that we did not show up.

"You said that we shouldn't say anything either. Right?" I wondered what he was trying to tell me.

"Yes, but we were going to be there," he explained.

"Oh, was that a mistake or something?" I really wondered. But I assumed if it was the medical records and the kids' statements to the police that they were concentrating on, no matter what recourse we took, they were going to indict.

I sat there across from Leggan for the next few minutes trying to convince him to take our case. He listened attentively. He said he would make a phone call on Gerald's behalf and the next thing I knew he was referring to Gerald as his client. I kept thinking, Gerald has a terrific lawyer, Leggan's got a new client, and we all have a strong case here.

The sparrows fluttered outside his window, while Mr. Leggan darted in and out of the office making plans for a not-so-sweet surrender. Another lawyer, recommended by a friend, had tipped us off that it was President's Day Monday. So I made sure Leggan was aware of it in case it mattered. I guess it did.

He set up the exchange for Tuesday morning instead, since he wanted to make sure the judge would be in. We would turn over Gerald and some money after a bond reduction hearing and they in return, would give back my husband.

So Leggan was hired. He proceeded to draw a map and tell me where we should meet him on that upcoming dreaded day. I would meet him at the door after spotting his red Mercedes. Gerald would stay behind in the car out in the parking lot.

He felt quite certain that the police didn't know what Ger looked like. I said, "Oh, they might." Little did he know that I had provided the prosecution team with family photos. He would have to be informed soon about my indiscretions. I didn't look forward to that.

"So I meet you first after I see you drive up. Then you'll tell me when to go and get Ger?" I confirmed our plan of action. We shook hands. I gave him a look of satisfaction and gratitude and said good-bye. I didn't look forward to Tuesday morning, but I was so glad Leggan was on our team now. Before leaving I did ask one more question, about the need to hide out until Tuesday.

He said, "Well sure, you have to. We want to stay in control here. We don't want them on your doorstep with handcuffs. You have until Tuesday. Find somewhere to stay until then."

Apparently it was the natural thing to do, get falsely accused of something, get indicted, make arrangements to surrender, hide out in the interim, and then walk in on a scheduled time and say, "You want me, here I am."

After I explained everything to Gerald, we rushed home to pack a few things. As we got closer to leaving, I began to get nervous, experience that feeling when you're just about out of the woods and at the last minute something happens to spoil it all.

Sure enough, we heard a knock at the door — a hard knock. I looked at Gerald and he looked back. We felt ruined, just what we wanted to avoid, an abrupt, offensive arrest. I asked, "Who is it?" Nobody answered. I utilized the peephole and could have sworn it was a plain clothes detective ready to capture Gerald. His head was turned so all I saw was the back of his head. He was a big guy in a large jacket with some grey hair at the base of his neck.

All of a sudden he pushed the door open. In walked my brother, Perry. We laughed like crazy, but I was still shaking with fear. Just like in the scary movies, the tension mounts and then it's not the real thing after all.

"You never open the door like that. How come you didn't answer when I asked who it was?" We stood in the living room discussing the situation.

"I didn't hear you say anything. I saw your cars and knew somebody had to be home. I got your calls on the answering machine but you wouldn't say what the problem was. I was so worried. Now what's going on around here?" He demanded an explanation.

I said I'd be happy to tell him along the way, but we were leaving before it was the real thing. I hooked Tiger to his leash and Gerald grabbed our overnight bags and my backpack.

"C'mon, let's go. The police could be showing up here any second, for all we know." We left the kitchen light on, climbed in our cars and drove off.

Gerald rode with Perry so he could fill him in on the details. I dropped Tiger off at Dad's, then headed for my other brother's house which would serve as our hide-out for the weekend. I made it clear to Rennie and Bonnie that as far as we knew they weren't aiding and abetting as long as arrangements had been made to surrender Tuesday morning with the proper authorities. They seemed comfortable with that.

"It's so peaceful and quiet here. I feel so safe in our little bedroom," I said to Bonnie. "I think we'll hide out here forever."

We began to feel right at home. I wondered if Anne Frank felt the same, comfortable among family and friends, yet fearful of the inevitable future confrontations with her persecutors. Although I knew her situation was much worse.

Their three-bedroom brick home with a basement and huge backyard seemed too big for the two of them but I guess they didn't mind the space. Both of their kids had gotten married, which left two bedrooms unoccupied, and one, for the time being, provided us a refuge. Our sleeping room contained a bed, dresser with a large mirror, a nightstand and an empty crib which their granddaughter used whenever she came to visit.

The crib was a stark, taunting reminder to Gerald and I that all of our diligent efforts put forth to have a child were producing nothing but failed attempts. Todd and Gerry's inclusion in our life meant so much to me. I was always grateful for their presence. It occurred to me that maybe they would be the only sons in my lifetime. If so, at least I would have them.

Ger told the story about Perry bursting in on us and how we thought it was the police. We all had a good laugh over it and other times we reminisced about. Then Rennie and Bonnie wanted to know more about what was happening concerning the indictment, so Gerald gave them an update. Since it was getting late, we decided to dine out at a pizza restaurant nearby and it was delicious.

After a while, Perry said he had to head on home but before he left I took him aside and asked him about the possibility of borrowing some money for the bond. Without hesitation, he generously agreed to help.

We spent the rest of the evening lounging around in the living room at my brother's house. The news came on. Ger and Ren discussed mostly sports, while Bonnie and I were more interested in the Harding-Kerrigan hot topic. Serious aspects of the nightly news reported an unusually high number of deadly fires lately in Kellton and all of us seemed to get a little edgy when a few politicians started hinting at the possibility of war.

As Gerald and I retired, it felt strange to be in totally different surroundings. We were lucky to have supportive family members who cared but I was so frightened at what might happen next. Before turning off the light after reading several pages in his book, Gerald didn't elaborate a great deal about how everything was affecting him, but he did mention the words "angry and embarrassed." He added, "I mean, I am really grateful. This is really nice of Bonnie and Rennie to let us stay here, but I sure wish it was under different circumstances."

I tossed and turned all night while Gerald slept like a baby, as usual.

The next morning, Rennie and I took a walk at the cemetery. I made the request since Mom was buried there.

After saying 'hi' to Mom, we took a walk along the bank of the creek which formed the east boundary of the cemetery.

"You see here, right there, that's all done by the beavers," Rennie said to me as we walked along.

"Oh yeah, I see all the trees are gnawed off. They blocked that all off like that?" I asked. "It sure looks like it," he said. "See how they are messing it all up. I think I'm going to fix it back to the way it was."

I told him that under no circumstances should he jump in the creek and undo the beaver's hard work, but he said he might. We kept our eyes open for the blue heron with a gigantic wingspan that frequents the pond near Mom's grave, but we figured it probably wasn't the right time of the year.

When we got back to Rennie's, the four of us mostly relaxed, conversed and joked about one thing or another. Gerald stayed strong and seemed to forget his dilemma for the time being, although time was running out.

Toward the late afternoon, however, he confessed that he didn't think he could follow through with a commitment which he had arranged at an earlier date. But he got dressed and decided to put in eight hours at the emergency room, after all.

I secretly worried all evening that maybe he put on his uniform in order to sneak off and drink his sorrows away for a while. It was only a matter of time, I assumed, before this mess would get to him.

He walked in shortly after midnight, as sober and proud as could be. Modestly and in one EMT or medical term or another, he explained how he had helped to save a life. The event obviously boosted his self-esteem. He slept well again. Of course, I didn't.

On Monday, our final night of visiting, we all sat around and watched more about 'Skatergate' and the rest of the latest Olympic wins and losses.

Everyone wanted to turn in early. I walked out to the car to get an extra pillow for the night. On the way back in I noticed the beautiful sky. It was clear for a change and I marveled at the bright stars and crescent moon.

Right here, Todd and Gerry, I wanted to assure them, Karrol and Dad are thinking of you and you are loved and greatly missed. I worried that they were probably staring out their window at home, wondering why we had disappeared.

Maybe too much time would elapse and one day they would no longer remember us. They were good at adapting. We certainly would never forget them and we would wait forever for our happy reunion.

The night hours passed on by until our free time was up. Gerald's precious liberties and privileges would soon be not only revoked, but what we considered violated.

Early in the morning, Bonnie and Rennie both wished us luck. We were on the road by 8 A.M., traveling toward the court house via the slow scenic route. Initially I parked at one of the other complexes, well out of sight, until we were ready to hold up the white flag.

We sat in the car for about ten minutes. Gerald didn't say much. He smoked instead. I tried to respond appropriately when he did ask about something.

It felt like we were in a fog on a train headed for disaster, a collision which would stop us dead in our tracks. We could try to get off the train at the next stop and escape, but we wouldn't be able to. Even if we did escape, then what?

I thought, today we can surrender to the law and put our faith in something good out there in the world which will eventually embrace us, or we can run toward a bunch of unknowns. Gerald and I both decided we were not going to take any shortcuts. In fact, the path called law and order seemed to be the slowest route toward justice, but we had to hope that, in the long run, it would prove to at least be the correct route.

Gerald and I understood somehow that our choices must be of the kind that we could live with. And in the end, hopefully, our choices would make us stronger, wiser and at some point, more able to make a positive difference in ourselves, our children's lives, and maybe even the world.

So on Tuesday, February 22, 1994, at approximately 9:15 A.M. in the morning, my husband stood ready to surrender to the Echo County jail in Crestwood Edge.

As luck would have it, the judge, the one he would go before for a bond reduction, wasn't in.

Therefore, it meant going back out there into the cold to prolong our odyssey or, as our entrusted lawyer put it, "We've got to get this thing started, but to do that, you've got to turn yourself in. Because if you don't, we're going to lose control of the situation, then it's in their hands, not ours. So we can't do anything until we start right here." He explained the necessity of surrendering as the three of us stood by our car shivering in the cold. "Now there's a chance we'll be able to inch our way in between something today, get the other judge to hear your plea for the bond reduction, but I think it's best we just go ahead and do this now, what do you think?" Leggan posed the crucial question to Gerald and awaited his decision.

"All right then," Gerald conceded, "let's do it. Let's go get it over with." He literally surrendered at that moment in time.

CHAPTER 11

Accompanied by his lawyer, Gerald walked toward a door that would soon close behind him and lock temporarily, but at least he would walk in with dignity. It was the only way an innocent person should have to surrender.

Upstairs, surrounded by the proper authorities and anticipating the injustice of it all, I wanted to stop it somehow, but I couldn't. I thought, before you humiliate my husband any more, could you please just stop this nonsense. We'll forgive you because you have been misled and do not know that you are making a terrible mistake.

Then the due process began. It resembled the Grinch stealing Christmas little by little. Gerald had to give up his wallet, his lighter, his comb, jewelry, including wedding ring. Right before my very own eyes, I witnessed the violation of an innocent man's freedom and dignity. Ger did what most men would do, tried his best to hold back the tears of sadness, anger and humiliation thrust upon him. But it didn't work. His eyes moistened and as they reddened, it became apparent that he felt abandoned by a justice system he wanted to believe in. For all practical purposes, they may as well have dragged him out to the field and burned his heart and soul at the stake right then and there. That's what it seemed like I was actually witnessing any way.

I placed my hand on top of his as it laid on the counter. "I'm so sorry you have to go through this, sweetheart. Please try to hang in there. This thing will be resolved. It's just taking much longer than we thought. Please don't give up." I said softly, "I love you."

Our lawyer explained that we would attempt to get a bond hearing set and see Gerald in a little while. Although Paul R. Leggan did his best, he explained the process to me as we stood outside a court room.

"Well, as God and luck would have it, you see all these people standing around out here?"

I knew bad news was coming. Nothing ever moved swiftly toward resolution.

"These people are jurors for a jury trial. So unfortunately, we're going to have to wait until 8:30 A.M. for Gerald's bond hearing. Now listen, I can maneuver some appointments around. I can be here for you guys, but it is going to have to wait until the morning."

He was probably wondering how well I was going to accept the par for the course bad news. I thought for a minute and then expressed my concerns.

"Maybe I'd better take some time to think about this, then I can call you." I conveyed my fears about letting Gerald stay in prison overnight. I thought about running around town trying to raise the rest of the money for the bail, because the idea of something happening just in one night, a fight or something, scared me to death. What if someone pulled a knife on him and killed him, then it would be all over. Maybe it was panic taking over, but all of my instincts were telling me to get Gerald out of jail before something happened.

"All right. Take some time then, but you have to call me if you bond him out. When you know what you're going to do, let everybody know because right now Gerald's expecting a bond hearing today." Leggan put his hat and coat on.

"Okay. I will. I'll let them know." Some choice, I thought, let Ger know he's destined to spend the night in jail or run around town like a crazy person and try to raise the rest of the money needed to bail him out.

I stood there in an Alzheimer-like numb state for a few minutes, hoping my mind would begin to function again — soon. Finally I came up with a next move and focused on some people to begin calling and asking for some help on the bail money.

In the meantime, I knew that Gerald needed to be informed of what was going on, so I wrote a note explaining that I would try my best to borrow some more money to pay the full bond. If I could get the money, I'd be back to bail him out. If not, he would have to wait until 8:30 in the morning for the bond hearing and Leggan would be here then and try to get the amount reduced..

I returned to the dark-haired man at the original arresting point to deliver my note to Gerald. "Well, your lawyer really should have come back here," he explained.

"Please, I just need to let him know that we couldn't get the bond hearing. He was thinking we would get that today. Could you at least just give him this note or tell him?" I pleaded politely.

He paused to consider the request. "Well, let's see. Come with me. I'll see what I can do." I followed and hoped as we walked down the stairs to the glass door which had a large sheriff's star painted on it.

As we walked in, I noticed a lady at the desk and two men standing there talking. One tall, practically bald guy joked with the man who had escorted me in. Referring to me as a potential prisoner, jokingly he said, "Hey pal, we usually sign in the prisoners upstairs." He laughed. It was obvious that the two of them knew each other.

I looked at him dead in the eye. "Usually I have a sense of humor, but not today." My facial muscles felt more serious and tighter than ever before.

"Oh boy." He suddenly realized that it was no time for jokes. "I take it this is no social call." He looked again at the man who had brought me in. After the gentleman handed him my note, it was dead silent in the room as he read it. All of a sudden he was the serious one.

"Okay. I'll take care of it."

After saying thank you, I turned to leave as the one gentleman opened the door, but I looked back and said, "We're going to win this one by the way."

I drove toward home in the cold and slush, listening to some music and trying to let it work therapeutically as usual in rough times like this. But at the time, Mariah Carey and all the rest had their work cut out for them.

As I came across a Pizza Hut, I remembered how handy the phones were, just inside the doorway. So I decided to try and contact a few people and humbly ask to borrow some money. The thought of it made my stomach churn, but I was so frightened about the thought of Gerald spending the night in jail.

I called a few relatives, two friends, and one person I never should have even thought about calling, but I wasn't thinking straight, just acting desperately. I knew I'd have to apologize later for my thoughtlessness. Anyway, nobody had much money to spare.

It felt good to be back home after the long weekend away. But something disappointing came to my attention right away. There was one message. There was no way to know how old it was. "Yes, Karrol. Listen," the female voice said, "it's 2:30 in the morning and there's a man standing behind your wagon right now. They've been pounding on the door here and I saw a squad car too. So I just wanted to let you know. Okay, this is Mrs. Rhoades. Bye."

I grabbed the phone, but couldn't remember her number offhand so I carried the cordless next door so I could find out what my neighbor was talking about. She told the story again about the other night.

And later that day, my other neighbors, Robby and Veronica, said they heard some pounding on their door too. "The cops said they received a call that shots were fired from here."

I wondered, were the police in active pursuit of Ger that night? Were they here to make the arrest and deny him his right to surrender peacefully as already planned? I hated the idea that they had disturbed all of our neighbors.

Whatever happened, thank God we missed it all. Once they showed up at our door, whatever the reason, we may have been subjected to another night of unnecessary grief. The warrant was valid. They would have taken him away.

I picked up Tiger and brought him home, then got busy on the phone calls again. As the evening wound down, I realized it was getting too late to try anymore. Hopefully, Gerald would survive. Large snowflakes began to fall and I could hear the wind whistling outside the bedroom window.

I cuddled with Tiger, lost myself in some music and tears and closed my eyes. The phone rang. After the beep, I could hear Gerald's voice. "Karrol, they took my cigarettes. Karrol? Are you there? You gotta get me out of here. Do you understand? Karrol, if you're there, c'mon, pick up. I'm not staying in jail. I want out of here. I'll call you back, or call me. Please. Bye. I love you."

My heart ached. His cries for help felt like whiplashes to my spirit. I couldn't help him.

Soon the phone rang again. This time I grabbed the phone. I said I'm sorry over and over. He promised that he would be all right until morning. He knew it was late and there was nothing more to be done at this point. He just wanted to make sure I was home and okay.

I crawled back into bed. My heart still ached. At least Gerald seemed safe. I tossed and turned all night.

By 5 A.M. I was awake and jittery, pacing like a carnival target back and forth in a shooting gallery. After a few minutes, I formulated the best plan of action that I could. I sat on the bed and counted every dollar we had and realized the 'Ger Fund' was definitely short. Some material things would have to go. I refused to leave the house without enough cash or collateral to bond him out. No more jail. Forget that. I had already failed one night.

I wondered, how much more of this either one of us could take, and I hoped Gerald wouldn't hate me for failing to get him released right away.

From the living room, almost afraid to, I peeked out the window. Snow had accumulated through the night. With the hazardous conditions, it would be difficult and slow getting to Crestwood Edge. I packed up the television and VCR, an expensive camera, my binoculars and some jewelry. I had approximately two thousand dollars in cash, more in checks, one last hundred in the bank, plus our material belongings, which I planned to pawn, if necessary.

"Hello, Rennie?" Although I was startled when the phone rang I was expecting his call. "Hi Karrol, it's Bonnie. Rennie's on his way but you know it might take him longer than usual with this mess."

"I know. This is unreal, isn't it? Is it still snowing there?" I asked.

"I don't think so, but we got quite a bit last night," she said.

"Us too. So he just left?"

"Yeah. Well, good luck today, and be careful. Call us later and let us know how it turns out." She yawned as she said the last few words.

"Okay, thanks. I'll call you tonight. Go back to bed," I suggested, then hung up.

I threw on some clothes and loaded everything in the car. Rennie plowed through the snow and ice and arrived around 7:30 A.M. He handed me some cash. I thought about how sweet and supportive he was, along with everyone else, throughout the whole ordeal. I gave him a hug and warned him to be careful on his way to work.

The road conditions were dangerous. The ice was beginning to melt but there were frequent slippery areas, still causing some drivers to swerve. Luckily I did not become one of the morning casualties I saw along the way. I kept thinking, I've just got to get there for him and Leggan.

I arrived at 9:30 A.M., a half hour late but everyone else appeared to be running a little behind too. Since I didn't have time to stop at the bank, I planned to stop off at the bank down the street from the court house later, if necessary. The pawn shop addresses were in my purse also, just in case.

Mr. Leggan and I smiled at each other as he entered the small room where the bond hearing would occur. He saw me counting the wad of money and asked how much I had. He counted it too, then told me to stick it safely back in my purse.

He hastily clued me in on a few details and guided me on some other important matters. I scanned over his bond reduction proposal and reasons for such, then sat down toward the back where Leggan pointed to.

I noticed that the proceeding judge was the same one who Leggan had spoken to yesterday, the one who had assured Ger the right to a bond hearing this morning. He had also acted like surrendering was a good thing, although it was still considered an arrest.

Before the hearing started, I searched through my purse and realized I did not have a pen, so I whispered to our lawyer. He came over and sat down beside me. He had an extra one in his left shirt pocket and let me borrow it. I looked down at the notepad which sat on his lap and noticed that he used his very own shorthand system. Many words and sentences were written in some sort of shortcut fashion. I saw some dates which referred to the alleged time periods, so I asked if he would write them down for me later and he said that he would furnish me with a copy.

A few more people entered the room, so Leggan took his seat at the table with the other lawyers. As I sat there observing the others, I guessed that only family members were allowed. One lawyer, I noticed, spoke with an Irish accent. He was instructing his client about something.

The judge exuded an aura of reverence. As he spoke, he appeared so dynamic and in control of everything. Down deep, my first gut feeling was that this particular judge was an honorable justice-seeker and pursuer of such. Unfortunately, I knew that he wouldn't be Gerald's judge for the criminal charges. That would be Judge Westley and we had heard that he was tough. Not that this one couldn't be. But, would Westley, the one who would decide our fate, provide us with justice in the end? I wondered.

Suddenly, the first shock wave hit me. The prisoners, my husband included, shuffled in, dressed in solid blue prison garb, sandals, and foot shackles. I hung my head and gasped, "Oh my God." I couldn't take the look of humiliation and grief on Gerald's face. He saw me and motioned with his cuffed hands as if to say, "Look what they've done to me."

Within minutes the whole next chapter of our nightmare got underway. Six prisoners lined up. I watched and listened in agony. The judge dealt with the prisoners one after another. Each time I heard Gerald's name I felt a spasm of disgust, disbelief, fear, and pain all at once.

There stood my husband, a man I had known and loved all these years, along with five other accused young men who were fighting for their life for crimes they did or didn't do. Several of them looked so lost, like young children who never had a chance or took advantage of a good opportunity

Yet Ger was among them. Even though he was motivated, hard-working, and innocent, he was facing forty years — forty years for something that never happened.

I said to myself right then and there, again, that Gerald would not spend one more day in jail.

I sat there mesmerized and disgusted. Following all of the questions and explanations, the other prisoners were ushered out by a guard who looked like he'd worked there too long. Gerald was the exception. He stayed for the prearranged bond reduction hearing. He was required to sit by the judge and look him square in the eyes.

The utter starkness of it all, I thought, as the recorder sucked in every word. The gray, spotted square blocks of cemented walls closed in on us. The surreal florescent lighting made me sleepy and caused faint shadows to discolor everyone's face.

The shelves full of law books purporting the mandatory promise and deliberation of law and order all reminded me, unfortunately, that my husband and I could not be pinched, awakened from our nightmare or saved from the pain any time soon. We would have to live through this hearing and probably many more court appearances, until we could prove Gerald's innocence.

Leggan began to speak. I listened and watched every minute of his smooth, succinctly presented discourse on my husband's behalf. He was a first class act. Dressed for success and ready to rock and roll, his true animated colors clearly brightened up the day. Paul R. Leggan, attorney at law; I could just imagine him interrogating Flora and calmly but methodically causing her story to fall apart.

The deputy prosecutor mumbled and fumbled around and when the judge gave him ample opportunity to say if the State agreed with the bond reduction, he responded, "No, I don't see anything here that says we agree with that." He didn't say the State disagreed. He barely got his passive words out. He did finally come up with the mention of how serious the allegations were. However, Leggan made it very clear that all Gerald wanted was his day in court to begin his defense, as well as offense in the matter. The accused, Gerald Karlin, would be there without a doubt.

Leggan was successful in accomplishing what we had hoped for, a reduced bond. The judge granted Gerald a two thousand dollar bond. I had hoped for even less, so we could return some of the borrowed money and make a car payment, but I was content and relieved.

Gerald was escorted away, but not before Mr. Leggan explained what would happen in the next hour or so in order to arrange for his release. Before we left the room, I tried to listen in while Leggan told the judge a quick story about something. I walked forward as they finished, thanked the judge and left.

Leggan put everyone in a good mood at the clerk's office. People were friendly again toward me. The dark cloud had blown away for awhile. As they all smiled and treated me with respect, I thought to myself, don't they know we're the bad guys? I paid the bond and obtained the papers necessary for Gerald's release.

I couldn't resist. So, as we stood out in the corridor, I asked Mr. Leggan if I could give him a hug. He said, "Sure." I complemented him on being a fine lawyer. Then we got down to business, discussing what had to be done right away and in the near future. I jotted down whatever I thought I needed to. After we finished up, I handed him back his pen. We said good-bye, and anxiously I headed for the jail.

Outside the jail, I sat on the hard bench and watched the clock tick while waiting impatiently. We had escaped the crisis mode, for awhile. I wanted to free my husband, pick up our dog from dad's and go home.

After the longest forty-five minutes, there he was in street clothes, smiling at me, walking away as a free man again, for the present. We hugged then walked quickly away, out into the cold and snow toward Dunn's for a burger and fries. There was no food at home in the refrigerator. The jolting contrast, I welcomed it, from a jail cell to dining out. My husband was back.

The waitress courteously served him coffee and referred to him as a respected 'Sir.' He joked with the waitress as usual.

He's like that with everybody, old or young, female or male, always personable, reaching out and relating. If only the judge could see him now, I thought, being his genuine self, and being treated with dignity and human courtesy, the way he deserved.

Gerald, Tiger and I lounged around all evening and it felt terrific. We watched Nancy Kerrigan look like she was skating right over to pick up the gold medal. She did her best, and personally I think silver is just as shiny as gold.

Our spirits were picking up. I felt my old positive self returning. I was glad Ger could go back to fulfilling his roles as husband, friend, father, CPR instructor, EMT, and pursuer of dreams, hopefully even, future paramedic.

Rennie stopped by after work. Gerald thanked him for his kind contribution to help post the bond and talked a little about his ordeal.

"Yeah, Rennie, saying I did this to my kids is like saying you walked right outside here and stole an elephant. Now you have the police looking all over, accusing you of stealing this elephant, but you know there is no elephant to be found. But you're guilty, anyway, because you have a history and it speaks for itself. They don't need any evidence." He expressed his frustration, but the tone of his voice didn't sound as angry as I thought it would. Rennie and I sat quietly in awe. "And I gotta tell 'ya," he continued, "I didn't feel very comfortable up there with all those child abusers. That's all they had up there, you know."

"Oh, you mean you were off in one certain section with just one kind of offenders, the child molesters?" I finally understood.

"Boy, that must have been an awful feeling," Rennie jumped in on the conversation.

"Oh yeah, that's all there was there, on that floor. And you know how in the prison movies everyone sits around and talks about what they did. Well here, nobody talked about it, except for me, of course. I guess my walking around talking about my being innocent didn't help them one bit. I mean, I know they were people too, that probably needed help a long time ago, but I don't know.

I guess the closest one guy got to saying he didn't do anything was this guy who said he got a hung jury. Then, you know what was funny, a lot of them seemed to have all of a sudden become great friends with God. Well, that's all fine and good, but a little late, I'm thinking." He paused for a moment and I wondered if he was done or not. Then he added, "No, I didn't feel good at all being there. I told them it was all a crock and that I was getting bailed out and never coming back." He laughed and acted like he was ready to take it all in stride. I kept thinking about how upset I'd be if somebody had thrown me in prison like that, knowing I was innocent.

After a little more visiting, Rennie braved the weather and road conditions again and headed for home. Gerald and I sat on the couch together watching one show after another, until we could barely hold our eyes open any longer.

He read a few pages and fell asleep while I laid there listening to some music by Bruce Hornsby. I recapped the events of the day. Mostly, I was grateful for the bond reduction. It would have been a crushing blow to receive a defeat so early.

I thought about Paul R. Leggan, the way he did his job so impressively today. And the way he told funny, meaningful stories that somebody told him a long time ago, ones he never forgot. I liked the graceful way he included me all day long, yet cautioned me about certain dos and don'ts.

Yet, I wondered why he couldn't grant me the credit advance we needed. I think it was the responsibility issue or something. He explained about his responsibilities toward others, everyone who works with him, how they expected to get paid. I could respect that, I just hoped we could pay him and the other bills that needed to be paid. We would find a way, because he just had to be there for Ger. That's all there was to it. I wished he could be even more flexible though.

Seeing Gerald off to work the next day was pure joy. His second night back, I gave him full smoking privileges for a week, but he didn't take advantage of my offer. He enjoyed the R.C. Cola and dark chocolate Milky Way I bought him, along with some homemade tacos. He rambled off some other favorite Mexican meal he'd like to have some day, but I didn't know what he was talking about until he spelled it for me. "R-a-n-c-h-e-r-o-s h-u-e-v-o-s. That's ranch eggs, it's like eggs over easy with some refried beans, and of course, you have to have tortillas with it. And boy, is it good."

I said, "Well, maybe one of your sisters could make it for you or we could eat out or something. All I know how to make is Americanized tacos. Sorry, that's the best I can do, Geraldo." I joked and called him by his full name, the way his father used to.

After supper, I offered to cuddle intimately, but he said that it was the furthest thing from his mind. I let him know that I understood, but it was so good to have him back, he had to share at least one long kiss and a few hugs with me.

He called it a night at 10:30, just following the news, while I stayed up and watched some television. I peeked in. He looked so peaceful sleeping on his side, at home, and safe, where he belonged.

In T.V. Guide, I ran across Jack Lemmon's version of 'The Days of Wine and Roses.' It brought to mind the conflict of interest within my life, living with a recovering alcoholic, and not wanting anything to do with destructive behavior. But, Gerald, a very lovable, giving person had wandered into my life five years ago and as soulmates do, we fell in love. I couldn't say no, and forfeit my belief in the power of love.

Eventually it worked and many happy years followed. We've had some rollercoaster rides even without this particular crisis, but I guess my husband and I figured out somehow, luckily, that our love and friendship is something special and deserves to be treasured and kept, forever. Today we are stronger than ever and we're certainly a team working together on a daily, life-long basis, for the welfare of the boys and other goals. That night on television, I decided to watch an old comedy instead. Gerald was home again and it felt great.

CHAPTER 12

A robin returned on March 11 and posed outside our kitchen window. I viewed the welcomed bird as a genuine reminder of the springtime of our lives. I hoped that soon warmer weather would help to make life brighter and easier.

Things were turning in our favor. Dr. Cobers' evaluation supported the truth, the fact that the kids were never molested by Gerald and most probably not by anyone else. Based on fact, not fiction, she provided material which supported the accurate, truthful conclusion.

Gerald and I were grateful and pleased with most of her report, with one exception, namely the 'slow-poke,' conservative approach she recommended toward reuniting with the kids. That disturbed us, the pace which was suggested to move things along so we could reunite with Todd and Gerry.

It was clear that the kids needed our help and they needed it quickly. Yet, apparently, even with proof that swift intervention was warranted, nobody would step in to help Todd and Gerry secure their safety and welfare or stop the mental abuse.

I suppose the element of proceeding with caution, again had something to do with it. Dr. Cobers did also mention the attachment that the kids had to their mother, Flora, and the fact that for some time they had been estranged from Gerald.

For Todd and Gerry's sake, she stressed the need for a gradual transition, rather than another shock to their vulnerable emotional state of being.

All things considered, Dr. Cobers was no doubt sincere and trying to help, yet remained firm on her own judgment call regarding how and at what pace to proceed. She showed concern for all parties involved and provided an honest, complete and caring report. That was her job, after all, not to play 'Custody Captain' and pick sides.

We came to the conclusion that there were no easy choices or quick solutions to our complicated problem. Prior to Father's Day, when visitation was initiated again, Gerald and I had supported the cautious, gradual phasing-in method for the boys' sake. However, at this point, in their best interests, we felt so strongly what they needed most was time, and lots of it, with a father who loved them dearly and a chance to learn the truth and live a more safe, happy and loving reality. We were so ready to give that to them, to see that they received the things they needed most at this crucial point in their young lives.

Ger and I had been enjoying our reprieve, until it was time to show up in court again. We were hoping for a dismissal since Dr. Cobers' report was done, but we didn't hear anything, so tensions mounted as the scheduled day for discovery arrived. We were notified a day earlier that Mr. Leggan would be tied up elsewhere in court, but a representative would substitute.

We stood outside the courtroom, looking downstairs, watching for our legal counsel. Finally he showed up. He walked right toward us and introduced himself as Paul R. Leggan, the second. He appeared young, small in stature, self-confident and resembled his dad. I told him so.

As we entered the courtroom chambers, it seemed so quiet and empty compared to other days. One female employee from the State sat ready to hand over their evidence. Two bailiffs who looked familiar walked back and forth as if they were looking for something. One of them joked, "We can't find the persecutor."

"Thanks a lot, pal," Gerald whispered, as we sat and waited impatiently for the discovery process to begin. Too bad Gerald and I couldn't have a sense of humor too, I thought. We would have to wait until this was all over.

We watched as one of the gentlemen assisted the judge with his robe. As court came to order and he sat down, the judge seemed to tower over all of us. As his name was called, Ger had to walk through the swinging half-sized door and stand before the judge with Leggan.

The first thing Leggan the Second did, was to hand Judge Westley something called a petition to excuse our attorney, since he had been called to court in Copperton and could not attend. It was funny because Paul Leggan stood there explaining why Paul Leggan couldn't be present. The judge joked about it after receiving a quick explanation. It made me feel good, for a second or two.

The discovery process lasted approximately four minutes. Gerald and I were dumbfounded. We thought our lawyer might get to speak for a few minutes and explain that the psychologist's evaluation was completed.

"Why are they continuing with this now?" Gerald and I both asked Leggan.

"Because that's our justice system," he answered.

I stressed the point that it wasn't a matter of simply believing that no abuse ever happened, it was something I knew for a fact. "Why do people refuse to listen to the fact that I was there?" Leggan merely shrugged his shoulders at my inquiry.

The three of us huddled outside the courtroom. We asked a number of questions, then all walked out together toward the parking lot. I longed for sunglasses because the sun beat down on the fields of snow and hurt my eyes.

"Hey hon," Gerald said as he turned the ignition on. "I have to stop by the Red Cross and pick up the Actar mannequins for the community CPR class I'm teaching tomorrow. You don't mind, do you, since we're so close?"

"No, I don't care, but say 'hi' to Jo Ellen, okay, because I don't really feel like coming in."

"Okay, I'll just run in and out." We both rolled our eyes, because we knew Jo Ellen would detain him for a while, in her efforts to persuade him to teach more classes.

Tiger was ready for his walk when we returned home, so my dog and I trudged through the melting snow for the next fifteen minutes. I thought maybe the walk would help clear my mind. It never failed though. I was soon dwelling over our situation.

Gerald went alone to the March 31st court appearance, since I didn't want to take off work any more than I had to. As assumed, it was the same deal, just a quick exchange. Our package of evidence was in their hands now, including the long list of witnesses I had compiled for Leggan. Many of their witnesses, especially health care workers, were the same people we wanted to talk to, so certain things could be brought out and substantiated or refuted. For instance, the issue about the boys drawing things which constituted something sexual. Dr. Cobers found that the boys had seen sexual materials and movies, something Gerald and I were unaware of, and yet, it was being claimed that they never had any experience with anything of a sexually explicit nature.

Gerald came directly home following the discovery session. When I got home from work, he was in fairly good spirits. I inquired about the turn of events for the day, but he explained that it was just like last time, a matter of handing over a package of information.

In the days that followed, he began to tire of working long hours and dealing with the crisis on a daily basis. I found another home health care case, but only part-time. I continued to search for a steady, full-time job.

Occasionally, we managed to feel like normal, everyday people living out our lives without all of the turmoil. On other days, however, we focused in on the reality of the pain and hardships which we faced, like court appearances and the stress of other matters.

In April of 1994, Ger and I returned to court and sat not more than a few yards away from Flora, his false accuser. The purpose that day was to obtain a jury trial date.

The huge Seal of Indiana which professed IN GOD WE TRUST hovered over Judge Westley. The colorful, patriotic state and country flags separated by the seal were impressive. On that day I stared forward and paid closer attention to the background behind the judge.

I zoomed in on the words, IN GOD WE TRUST. Saying the words to myself made me feel like a hypocrite because I wanted to believe that God would be there for us and the kids, and find us some way out of this mess. But because the nightmare had dragged and on and on, with each passing day, my faith had weakened.

Court was in session. Family members took the stand one by one and pleaded for leniency for a related female first offender criminal. One aunt, especially, eloquently beseeched the judge on behalf of her niece, to be kind and go easy on her. The criminal got six years instead. Following the stiff sentence, the painful screeches and sobbing echoed throughout the corridors of the courthouse building.

We waited, hoping Gerald would be next so we could get it over with. I glanced up again and thought about what the word God means to kids. I knew whenever I tried to explain the concept of God to my nephew it was difficult. It occurred to me that parents are the ones in children's lives who mean so much. It's the mother or father who they see every day, the people they can touch and trust to be there for them that they can understand and believe in. The concept of God only comes later for young children.

The bailiff with the receding hairline, a Nixon look-alike, was present at our other hearings. As he walked by me, I inquired about the judge.

"Oh yes," he said assuredly, "he's a fair judge. If you've got it coming, he'll give it to you. But he tries to abide by the truth and he is fair."

Apparently the young lady who chose to sell drugs had it coming to her. Ger and I both wanted to believe that Judge Westley would determine the truth, that Gerald certainly did not have it coming to him!

"And what is the answer to the question? What is your defense in the matter of Gerald Karlin on the two felony counts of child molestation?" the judge asked matter of factly as he pushed his glasses upward and stared at our lawyer.

"Yes, your Honor, it's simply a contrived case by the mother to deny my client visitation with his sons." Paul R. Leggan, our attorney, stated as succinctly as he could.

It all happened within minutes. The next thing we knew, a date was set for a jury trial in October. Since our business was done, we abruptly left the courtroom. Gerald, Mr. Leggan and I walked down a corridor and sat on a hard bench to discuss vitally important matters.

Downstairs, family members of the convicted drug seller were still crying and trying their best to console each other.

"If it were any other kind of charge, I'd say yes, Gerald, think about a plea. But not this. Because you want to see your kids again, have them be a part of your life, right?" He paused.

Ger gave a quick nod. "Absolutely."

"Right, well, that's what I thought. Now like I said, they'll be sending me a letter and it might say something like, oh, you just fondled the kids. But again, I'm telling you, if you admit to anything at all in that courtroom or on paper, you'll never see your kids again."

The three of us sat closely huddled together and listened intently to everything said.

"Well, I'll say it again, I'm not admitting to anything I didn't do. I'm innocent. They can threaten me, whatever. I just want them all to listen to the truth for once." Ger stood firm in his initial convictions about the whole senseless ordeal.

"Well good." Leggan smiled. "And I respect you for that. So now what we have before us is the task of showing reasonable doubt. Now I'll tell you, there's an enormous amount of work to be done. I asked for the later jury trial date so we could have a long time to prepare. Besides, the court's also got a lot of cases to hear before yours." He continued to fill us in on certain important points.

I noticed he was dressed for success again as usual. This time Paul wore a green silk handkerchief to top off his three-piece suit. Every sandy blond hair was combed neatly in place, even though he wore a hat as he came and went. He was polished and professional, yet friendly, somewhere in the middle of his life span, I guessed. As he spoke, Ger and I sat waiting to hear what amount of money we had to miraculously come up with to pay for the big event, the jury trial.

Then he said it. But he prepped us first with a warning. "Now I don't propose how you're going to or if you can come up with this kind of money, but, okay are you ready for this?" He waited for a second or two. "We're probably talking about ten to fifteen thousand dollars."

Gerald and I exchanged a quick glance. Then I said seriously, "But Paul, we just don't have that kind of money." I added facetiously, "What bank do you suggest we rob?" Leggan managed a grin. Gerald acted so calm and just remained quiet. I didn't know quite what to think. But I knew I would hear his thoughts on the outrageous amount soon enough.

102

Leggan acknowledged that it would take us some time to figure out what to do at this point. Then he explained that once he negatively replied in answer to the prosecution's query concerning a plea bargain, that it was at this point in time that he would be locked in as our lawyer. Leggan guessed that this would occur around June. So in essence, most of the fee would be due then.

I, for one, was flabbergasted. According to previous estimations, I was more prepared for something like five to eight thousand dollars and the possibility of paying over a period of time. We were broke already. It was a bleak moment in time, still wanting to believe in some monetary miracle but ultimately realizing that soon Paul R. Leggan, the fine attorney who I had more or less considered to be a guardian angel of sorts, would no longer be on our team.

"I've always hated the cliche, but there I sat thinking it. "Who ever said life was fair?"

Since November of 1992 when we finally got the papers started, all we ever wanted was our day in court. We wanted to continue to be parents to Todd and Gerry. And yet after our initial eight to nine thousand dollars and now another seemingly insurmountable amount, we still had to wonder. Would anyone ever listen to the facts, the truth? We thought that maybe we were actually just wasting money and paving the way for Gerald's nightmare in a jail cell for some awful thing which never happened.

All of a sudden I heard Gerald say, "Does this happen a lot? I mean, I'm curious, does this happen in divorce cases very often?"

"Well, as a matter of a fact, I have twelve cases similar to this one right now. So it seems to be happening more and more," Leggan answered.

Ger continued, "The thought that a parent could sacrifice their own for some grudge or sense of control over an ex-spouse. It's not right, the kids being used as pawns. And what really gets me, I know I've told you this often, Karrol, is Flora said she'd never keep the boys from me."

I nudged Gerald softly, then blurted out an idea that popped into my head. "Is your son a lawyer?"

Leggan nodded. "Yes he is." He looked at me as if to say, you know he is because he had to show up here for me as proxy on a previous occasion.

"Well, do you think he could represent us, would that be a possibility? And how much would a bench trial be, that would save us some money too, wouldn't it?" Gerald and I tuned in for his reply.

"I guess that'd be something for you to consider. And a bench trial, oh, I'd say it would probably run you about eight thousand." Then he quickly changed the subject back to himself as attorney and explained that, "Gerald's very best chances for a finding of not guilty are with a jury."

We were told to think it over and let him know our decision as soon as possible. But for now, he didn't want anything to interfere with the opposition sending him the plea bargain letter. He could withdraw at a later date if it was necessary.

We stood up ready to say our good-byes for the day and Ger said, "Well, we won't string you along. We'll let you know soon. But listen, thanks for everything so far." We both shook his hand. He picked up his briefcase, coat and hat and left.

Gerald and I exited the courthouse dazed and astounded. I can't say more than ever before, but it was certainly another jolt to our senses. "Ten to fifteen thousand dollars," we kept repeating louder and louder to each other as we walked toward the car.

We had spent every penny already and more, by borrowing, just to get to the point we were at, some type of unfair crossroads which seemed like nothing more than another frustrating beginning. And now we had to sit and wait another five months or so. It was April. The trial wouldn't begin until October.

The ride home was an unusually quiet one, considering the circumstances. We were both doing some hard thinking. We'd exchange a token pat on the leg or tender "I love you" every so often. But then comments turned to, "What are we going to do?" Mostly, we were emotionally numb again from the unfairness and seemingly hopelessness of it all.

As we neared home, we both simultaneously expressed the heart-breaking realization that we were going to have to move. We knew it was the only way we could manage. Bills kept piling up and a few important payments were behind. We couldn't come up with the kind of money Leggan quoted. Unless it was on a monthly basis, we couldn't really even think about paying lawyers any more.

The stress of moving began to monopolize my thoughts as we drove the last few miles home.

In the next few days, we used our telephone as much as we could since we knew before long it would be a convenience that wouldn't be there anymore. Gerald surprised me and began to make some of the calls himself. He thanked me over and over again for all of the time I had spent on his behalf and explained again how he had simply tried to block it all out, in order to merely function. He said it didn't make any sense that the court was continuing to pursue the ridiculous matter, since Dr. Cobers' report was in and supported the truth, the fact that no abuse occurred.

We inquired to various sources regarding what steps to take to set in motion Dr. Cobers' recommendations, but it seemed no matter where we turned, the answers were the same and not what we wanted to hear. Supposedly, we could only wait until the charges were dropped. Nothing could or would be done until then. And to be honest, we were still consumed by the fear that even now, nobody would listen, especially the prosecutors.

CHAPTER 13

Within a week's time, we had hosted a moving sale and unloaded what seemed like tons of accumulated junk. Many items were only worthy of a toss in the garbage can, but we also sold some valuables. We suffered the heartache that packrats feel when parting ways with useless, but sentimental favorites, as well as more expensive belongings, such as a nineteen-inch RCA color television Ger had won in a raffle for a single dollar. We needed the money.

Finally, the garage, closets, and attic were empty. Unfortunately, the cozy yellow two-bedroom house on Sarasota Street didn't belong to us, but it certainly felt like home. The last of the boxes were stacked up in the living room. On April 30th, we spent our last night reminiscing and anticipating changes we really had no desire to make. The thing that worried us most was our impending infringement upon others and our own loss of privacy.

Gerald pulled the comforter over his chest, then opened his book. I paused and took one last sentimental look at the bare walls and blue curtains before turning off the overhead light. A small crystal lamp and foam mattress makeshift bed would have to suffice for the night. For five years we slept and woke up together in this room, I thought to myself. We shared dreams, secrets, joys and sorrows as all couples do.

I crawled under the covers beside my husband. We were both exhausted. For the entire week we did little else in the evenings but clean and pack. During the day, we struggled through work. I had answered an add in the paper and was lucky enough to secure at least a short-term full-time job.

We were short on sleep and my allergies and asthma had flared up to make things more uncomfortable. I relied on three pillows to help prop up my head for better breathing.

"Do you have enough light, hon?" I asked.

"Yeah, it's okay, but listen, I'm gonna smoke one more, all right? I'll be right back." As he stood up slowly, his knees made a slight popping sound. After I heard the kitchen door open, I envisioned Gerald savoring one last mental picture of the good times we enjoyed in the backyard with the kids.

A clothesline had served as a badminton net. Teams consisted of little Gerry and myself against Todd and Ger. We barbecued, played a lot of catch and even pitched a tent at times. The back gate opened to a gravel alley which led to a wooded area. The kids, Tiger, and I took frequent walks. I always had to yell at the boys to put the sticks and rocks down.

As I laid there, the drawbacks of moving came to mind. That restless, uneasy feeling of being unsettled would surely begin to haunt us. The saddest part of all would be the loss of a friendly, quiet, familiar neighborhood, and a sense of belonging and place to call home.

During the walk home from work earlier, I had thought about the calls to cancel the phone, utilities, cable, the newspaper. Every action seemed to sting and cast doubts on our decisions and uncertain future.

It was evident that our stay here would soon be history. I didn't anticipate being courageous enough to pass by the street where we used to live, for a long time.

Within minutes, Ger laid back down and put his arm around me at the waist. "God, I'm going to miss this place."

"Me too, sweetheart. We have so many good memories here."

"Five years almost of married life, and some great times with the boys," he reflected.

"Yep, and I'll never forget it either. We'll find another cozy place like this someday. We will." I was tired but not defeated, and struggled to say something optimistic. "I hope so. Well listen, here's the deal. I'm going to read a few more pages and that's it for me. I'm beat. And we have to haul the rest of that stuff over to storage and your Dad's tomorrow. So good-night." He kissed me on the cheek and rolled over on his right side.

"Good-night. I love you," I whispered.

"I love you too. I'll probably run down to Dunkin Donuts in the morning and get some coffee. I'll bring you your usual, okay?" He knew that meant two plain cake doughnuts and a small container of milk.

"That'd be great." I patted him on the back. Then he delved into some sort of sci-fi imaginary world.

The story I was reading provided some relief too. Remembering the movie with Sally Field, I bought the book one day thinking if mother and daughter could survive such an unbelievable, ghastly nightmare, then maybe father and sons could experience a happy ending too.

Yet, every time we turned around things seemed to get more frightening, especially with the reality of a trial looming in the future.

I wanted so badly to sleep and wake up without constant worries, but nights were difficult and my mind always raced rather than rested. I stared at the pages before me. After an hour or so of contemplating, it was necessary to get up and go to the bathroom. As an aid to alleviate my headache and help me try and get some sleep, I swallowed two Tylenol.

On the way back, I peeked into the boys' room. Before I took down all of their wildlife posters and eleven by fourteen Y.M.C.A. photos, I snapped some pictures, hoping that someday Todd and Gerry would be lucky enough to remember and experience the proper flashbacks regarding their room and life here with their father.

It was the best I could do, because tomorrow we would have to leave. I laid back down under the covers. It was the dead of the night and quiet except for the snoring of Gerald and my dog, which I was used to.

I'm trying to focus in on the judge, but I can't. Maybe if I rub my eyes. Oh, here's Katie, to my left. Look at that long, bushy golden brown hair. And there's Gin and Jonathan, with his blond hair. What a contrast. His hair is so long. She only lets me cut the top and sides. Oh good, Dad is here, along with my two brothers. Who's that lady sitting next to Perry? She looks so much like Mom. But where is Gerald? Oh, there he is, to the left of the judge. I'll rub my eyes again. Maybe I can get the blur out to make out if it's Judge Westley. I should have worn my new glasses.

Oh God, there they are. "Todd, Gerry, I love you." Finally I got to tell them. I hope they could tell what I said. Gosh it's good to see them smile. They're still not as tall as I thought they might be by now. "Katie, Katie, look." I reached over and tapped her on the shoulder. "There's Todd and Gerry smiling and waving at us."

I squinted to see as they faded out of focus. And there's Flora, of course, sitting next to them. That's odd. Her hair, it's bright red. I thought it was black.

Where are Ger's sisters? And Lucy and Sanford, they should be here. Maybe their van wouldn't start again. Oh no, where is Dr. Cobers with her poster board? She promised to be here. Who are all these strangers? They keep whispering. Why are they doing that? They are not supposed to be able to do that. I'm going to tell the judge to make them all stop it. He'll pound his gavel and yell, "Order. Order in the court!"

There he is, the Nixon look-alike bailiff. Oh, there's the judge. I don't think it is Westley. He looks more like Santa Claus with that white hair and beard. But he isn't smiling.

What's that? Oh, one of the jurors, he sneezed. There are only six of them, all in white uniforms. They sure look serious.

"What the heck's going on, now where's Gerald? Now don't panic, just stay calm."

"Shh, Aunt Karrol, be quiet. Shh." Jonathan put his index finger to his little lips and instructed me.

"Oh, sorry." The court room looks about the same, the seal, the platforms for defendants and witnesses to speak from, the rows of chairs that we can sit in so we can watch.

"Bring the prisoner in." I heard someone yell.

I began to whisper. "Whose voice was that? Where is Gerald? What's that awful clanking sound? There he is. Oh no, he's got those wretched chains on his ankles again."

Katie heard me. "I see. Look Karrol, it's the boys, they're getting up and running over to him."

"Good. Finally they get to see each other, after all this time. Those poor guys, look at them, just clinging to his pant legs. I don't know if Ger's gonna be able to handle this. I need some Kleenex. I can't stand it. They look so happy. It's good to see them happy. Oh geez, I think I'm gonna be sick."

"Don't cry, Karrol, see, it's going to be just fine. There's no way in the world Gerald abused those boys. They'll see that now."

"I hope so, Dad. But what if they find him guilty? What are we going to do?"

"You just hang in there. Everything will turn out just fine. Now look. I think they're going to let him talk now."

"Yes, your honor. I am innocent and I love my kids. That's all I have to say. Nothing more, nothing less."

I woke up coughing and darted straight up in bed. I ran to the bathroom to get some water. If I didn't get some immediately, I felt like I would die. "Oh God, please God, just let it all be over with. Please just make it end."

The choking sensation continued and my stomach felt worse than in the nightmare. "I never feel safe anymore," I mumbled to myself. "It's just a dream. It's just a dream, a nightmare." Why can't it all just be over with? I wondered. Once again, I felt like closing my eyes and never having to open them to the sad reality which we were being forced to endure. I washed my face with a cold washcloth, got dressed and prepared to live another day in limbo.

As I sat in the kitchen on a folding chair with my feet propped up on the windowsill, I watched a squirrel bury some peanuts that Gerald had set out.

Gerald finally got up. "Good morning, what time did you wake up?"

"Oh, a while ago, about seven, I guess," I answered.

"Hey, honey, you want to really confuse Rocky, our poor little squirrel friend?" I joked. "Go out there later, just to the left of the tree by the picnic table and dig up his food. Then we'll watch his reaction when he comes back for it. He'll say, 'now I know I hid it right here'."

We both laughed but then realized we wouldn't be around later to watch him dig it up.

"You're too cruel. So that's what you're watching, huh?" He stood behind me and put his hands on my shoulders. "Hey, let me run down and get me that coffee and our doughnuts, okay?"

111

"Sure, and when you come back, I have to tell you about a dream that woke me up this morning."

After he returned, I told him all about my dream, except for one thing. I had the judge and jury saying, "Mr. Karlin, you're free to go. Sorry about all this."

From nine to nine-thirty, Ger and I made a few last phone calls before we packed up the phone. Our friends and family were naïve like us and figured it would all be over by now. They asked repeatedly why the case was being pursued and why we couldn't see the boys, now that the evaluation supported Gerald's innocence. It was another million dollar question and we had absolutely no answer for them. We were totally bewildered why the lawyers, judges, child advocates and court system had no answer for us.

By 11 A.M. both cars were loaded with the rest of our belongings. Tiger and I took one final walk down the alley. Then I squeezed him in the little space remaining in the front seat. Gerald and I quickly walked through the house one last time. We locked the door and drove off.

CHAPTER 14

So we piled in with my father, sister, her boyfriend, their kids, and a character named James, a truck driver friend of Dad's who came and went, and slept on the couch downstairs when he was home.

Unfortunately, Dad had cracked his tailbone one night as he fell. He already had trouble getting around, since his left leg remained weak from a mild stroke two years prior. But he took his physical decline in stride and said he'd survive.

Consequently, Gerald and I were offered his bedroom upstairs for the time being. As he recovered, which would take about six weeks, and when the hot temperatures began, we understood that he would need it back, since the air conditioner was in his window. In place of a twenty year old sofa, we donated our two-cushion, rust-colored velour sofa, hide-a-bed. Dad consented to sleep on it in the living room.

It was hectic at first, dealing with the stress of losing our own place. I tried, but wasn't much fun to be around for the first week. Especially difficult were the times when Ger and I went out in the evening for a while only to return feeling awkward and hurt. Everything felt strange. After two hours at Dad's, it seemed like we should leave and return home after the visit, yet that is where we lived, for the time being.

We adapted to the family and they adapted to us, I guess. We had to carry Tiger up and down the stairs. That was difficult, but we did it, every morning and every night. I hand fed him too. I found a courtyard nearby at a school, so he could walk freely at times, since it was fenced in. It was great being around my nephew and Rick's daughter. They always helped to take my mind off of things for a little while.

One day in the mail, we received a reply from our lawyer. The idea of letting Leggan the Second, an inexperienced lawyer try Gerald's case, had been discussed, but not accepted. The fee remained at fifteen thousand dollars, since we had already paid him two thousand dollars.

113

We soon found out from Mr. Leggan that Gerald would have to attend court even for the purpose of accomplishing our lawyer's withdrawal. I asked him to reconsider one last time one day as we spoke on the telephone.

"It would be nice if you would reconsider and see this through with us, Mr. Leggan." I hinted without much hope.

"Well, it would be a matter of economics," he answered honestly.

"I know. For us too." I said. "I'm trying to get this lawyer in Kellton to take the case and let us pay on time."

"From Kellton? Don't you have any there in Indiana?" he asked.

"I guess so, but he's like you, works a lot in divorce cases, with father's rights, you know," I explained.

"Oh, I see. Okay. Well, good luck. And tell Gerald I need to see him soon, before we go to court, okay?"

"I will. Talk to you later. Good-bye." It hit hard, the reality that soon we would be alone again in our fight. I thought about how guardian angels are supposed to be able to work miracles and look beyond money at times. But it was just another grown up fact of life. When on Earth, some guardian angels do as the earthlings do, and money comes first.

Gerald and I realized that we had to either find a lawyer who would take payments, or attempt to secure a court-appointed one. We simply did not have any more money.

As the one steady job ended, I continued to work at Lucy's on the weekend's and another home health care job. Life went on in the midst of our relentless crisis, with all of the lulls in between phone calls and court dates concerning the matter.

One morning, through squinting, half open eyes, I noticed the digital clock numbers read 6:30 in the morning.

"Go get your diaper changed!" Dad yelled loud enough to wake everyone. "And Jon, you need some socks on!" Noise traveled well from downstairs to the upstairs. I turned on my right side to try and alleviate the back pain obtained from a soft mattress and there lay Gerald with his eyes wide open.

"Oh, hi. You're awake too?" I acknowledged.

"Yes, I'm awake." He didn't sound too happy about it.

We closed our eyes again and tried to go back to sleep for another half hour, but as we heard the kids clumping up the stairs, we realized it was useless.

Just as I was leaving for work, Dad relayed some sad news. "By the way," he said, "Jackie Onassis died; died yesterday in her own apartment, I guess."

"Oh no, really? That was fast, huh?" I said sadly. A chill ran through my body reminding me of the day I heard about President Kennedy's assassination.

"Yep. Cancer. Sixty-four years old." He scooted forward on the couch in order to make it easier for him to stand up. He finally stood up, got his balance and went to the kitchen to fix himself some toast.

After returning upstairs to give Gerald a kiss good-bye, I peeked around the kitchen corner and told Dad I'd see him later, and left for work. While walking to the car, I thought to myself, another legend lost to cancer.

It was a long day, because I had to work two hours overtime since a nurse needed me to fill in for her. While lying next to Gerald in bed that night, he told me that he couldn't get the house off his mind today.

"I know, I miss it too." Then I changed the subject. "Did you see the article in the newspaper about the forum on sexual abuse, do you wanna go, give it a try? I think we should go. Maybe we'll get in touch with someone, at least get a name, a contact, someone who might listen to our side, help the kids, which in turn would help you too. Somebody's got to listen and start helping us and the kids." I kept rambling on.

"Well," he said, "I knew you'd want to go if you saw that article. But, Karrol, why don't you go, because I'm afraid if I go, I'll just get too discouraged or blow up at someone if they won't listen. Honestly honey, I don't think I should be there, really. I'm trying to devote more time and energy to this, but I just don't think I should go to this thing. I know it will get to me and then I will be miserable for the rest of the day. I don't want to ruin this day. Right now, I've got to just hope for the best on my case and deal with it a day at a time. You know what I mean?" He looked at me and hoped I understood.

"I know. I know. You just keep surviving and believing, okay, but I want to go. It might help. I just don't want to miss an opportunity. After the forum, we can still take our ride to the country. We'll still have time. How does that sound?"

"That sounds good, hon." He added, "And if we do find something for rent, we can move and I'll find a job down that way. A yearning to move to the country had begun to gnaw at us both. My mind was made up about attending the forum, so he agreed to sit in the car while I checked it out. When it ended, we planned to drive south and see what we could find.

He gave me a hug and told me how much he appreciated all I tried to do. But throughout our ordeal, I always felt like everyone involved, including myself, should have been doing more to end the unnecessary turmoil.

The alarm clock rang at 7:30 A.M. Slowly, but surely, I made myself presentable and headed for Sappho's to xerox a bunch of papers before attending the forum. The first page read:

PLEASE HELP

My husband, a loving father, has been falsely accused. These charges were filed approximately eight months after he initiated a court fight to restore his long term, liberal, involved visitation rights as a parent. Our justice system and child protection services are failing miserably in this case which should be working to protect the innocent, a father and two damaged sons. Sometimes fathers are innocent. Yet, nobody will help. Please hear our side and stop the unjust abuse and violation of abuse laws meant to protect children!

Signed,
Mr. and Mrs. Gerald Karlin

The informative package also contained the essay I had written on protecting the innocent and an article entitled, "Child Sex Abuse: True or False?" written by Dr. Domeena C. Renshaw. In the article, she tries to educate physicians, child therapists, lawyers and teachers regarding the increase in the use of false allegations as weapons in divorce/custody disputes. A few other items of importance were also included along with a detailed report of our costs to date, which totaled approximately ten thousand dollars. I wrote, "There are no words to describe the emotional costs." Each member of the forum panel would receive our package in hopes that someone would help. It took awhile at the store that morning to make the copies, collate and staple them. By the time I returned, Gerald was ready to go, but it was getting late.

Around 10:00 A.M., while Gerald waited in the car as planned, I tiptoed into the small room across from the library at the university as an important department head spoke. I found a seat and began to listen and look over the speakers.

God, I don't want to leave here today feeling frustrated and hopeless, I thought to myself. I tried to get in the right frame of mind, because I knew the right attitude and prepared questions were vitally important if I hoped to achieve anything positive. I sat and listened as a concerned individual.

Approximately thirty-five adults were present, most of them dressed professionally. A few concerned parents also seemed to be looking for some answers. The video presented that day, "Only in the Shadows," had apparently just ended. The blue, blank television screen remained on. A wall clock generated a buzzing sound as I tried to focus on the soft-spoken woman's words. My first impression was that maybe she would be the one to help.

Her gray, curly, shoulder length hair gave the impression of age, yet her demeanor exuded a youthful nature. Only one florescent light out of many flickered. A panel of three other women sat at the tables before their audience as this particular representative spoke.

The conference room was decorated with the usual collegiate style pastel paintings. The walls were a dull gray shade but the red and white carpet added some color. We all sat in rows of blue folding chairs, looked straight ahead and listened attentively.

The atmosphere made me feel comfortable and safe, yet skepticism still tugged at my heart. Too many disappointments had occurred already. Ger and I both knew that we had to get the ball rolling in our direction before we stepped into that mess of a jury trial in October. We had to make someone listen and get Todd and Gerry the proper help.

"In Ohio, for instance, they have four thousand case workers," the woman said. "In Indiana we only have five hundred and we lose six hundred thousand dollars every year to Illinois simply because we keep the words 'serious risk' in the books. It's been a law since 1979, but we feel it's important. Indiana does require that anyone report abuse, but we feel it is important, not just mandatory people like the law enforcers or teachers, etc." One interesting fact after another rolled off her tongue. "So Indiana isn't in the greatest shape, but we're doing better on some things than many other states."

She explained more about the budget, some goals for 1995, touched upon the registry issue, and two opposing concepts, child safety versus reuniting abused children with their parents after intervention. "Surprisingly, so often kids taken away and put in foster homes wind up with no sense of belonging or permanence. And at the age of eighteen, they return to their own parents anyway, despite the history of abuse."

I learned that although the train of thought supporting reunification continued, many of the experts wanted to begin to stress child safety again, since they feared that maybe everyone had bent top far in the other direction. The speaker made it clear that the child's welfare was certainly always the primary goal, but the concept needed to be emphasized again. She wrapped up her speech with comments I had longed to hear and see someone act upon.

"We're here to help, but we need everyone in this room to help too. And it's our duty, our duty, to investigate and help whenever we can." Finally it was time for questions.

Today, after so long, I would get to ask a question that had nagged at our family for so long. Patiently, I waited as the good-looking slim university fellow who called himself the 'Agenda

Policeman' selected one person after another to ask a question. My hand went up and down.

A long-winded lady, looking for some answers like the rest of us, passionately wanted to know this and why that. Some things just did not make sense as far as she was concerned. She began to get on my nerves slightly, because I knew time was running out. Others still had to speak.

Another middle-aged man who worked in the coroner's office questioned the validity of all the money spent on computers. "I mean, is it really going to help?" he asked. "We need workshops, we need parent-teacher classes. These kids are hurting and out of control, along with many of the parents." He spoke vehemently about his concerns: burnout, a sense of hopelessness, lethargic parents and lost children. 'A society in crisis,' is the way he described it.

The optimistic and helpful speaker answered with the notion of trying to give kids hope and she reiterated the concept that the parent is the first teacher. "So many ills of society could be prevented if only some parents were better parents," she stated. She continued and defined family with a modern definition. "Family, these days, defines itself and includes foster parents, adoptive parents. It's all inclusive. We no longer think in terms of a nuclear, normal family of any one kind."

I looked the agenda policeman in the eyes as I held up my hand again. As soon as he acknowledged me, I stood up. Here goes, I thought. "Yes, uh, according to a great deal of research, and for one a psychiatry professor at Loyola University, Dr. Domeena Renshaw, it's become more and more popular to use false sexual abuse claims as a weapon in divorce cases involving custody fights. The false claims are used so one parent can try and win sole custody and deny the other parent any visitation. What is done in these cases to first, assure an impartial, two-sided investigation, and two, to make certain the accused parent is treated innocently until proven guilty?"

I was surprised that I had managed to ask exactly what I had planned to. But my knees felt shaky as I finished and sat down. I kept looking at her for the answers.

She acknowledged right away that the divorce/custody issue is sometimes a bad situation with parents thrusting war upon each other and using their kids as ammunition. "In the news," she noted, "there have been some bitter cases. And of course, it's the kids who suffer." She looked directly at me as she spoke. "Now to answer your questions, sometimes in cases like that, when it's known a custody case is going on, a mediator is brought in to listen to both sides."

Then she got off the track, as far as Gerald and I were concerned. She explained that if compelling evidence existed, sometimes the proper authorities simply moved forward to pursue prosecution. I thought about the medical records, how biased they were, and Gerald's history with alcoholism, how it all probably added to their compelling evidence.

I tried to keep my mouth shut, but finally had to interrupt. "But what if no one listens to one side at all? I know of a case in particular where nobody will listen to the father's side of the story, even though he was trying to legally secure visitation." But she just reiterated the concept of compelling evidence and mentioned again how kids involved in divorce cases are caught in the middle.

Another member of the panel interjected before the speaker could respond to the 'innocent until proven guilty' part of my question. "Let me just add that in cases of malicious filing of charges, when they're not in good faith, there are laws to protect against the false charges. Then it becomes a crime, a misdemeanor."

As she spoke, I kept thinking, I'll be contacting you June 1st, when the new youth center opens up. I had read an article about the center and saw her picture. She'll definitely receive one of our plea packages today before I leave.

The last two speakers told about their affiliation with certain agencies and spoke briefly on other aspects of child abuse. Then as expected, the members of the panel were asked to stay over for a few minutes for any final questions.

Again, patiently waiting behind a few people, feeling a sense of relief that the experience was laid back and might prove useful, I readied the stapled papers for the four of them. Mostly

120

today, though, I wanted so badly to walk away with a name and a contact.

I chose the first speaker, the most powerful one, a department head from Cardinal City, to briefly explain our dire need of help. "Yes, hi, if you could read this first page, then maybe we could talk for a second." She took it in her hands and read from the paper. She turned to the second page which began with my essay, Protecting the Innocent. Then she began to ask questions and gave me a chance to explain a little more about our situation in a speedy fashion. She seemed genuinely interested and honored me with what I had come for.

"I do have someone, her name is Leslie Lassiter. I think I'll have her look into this." She placed my package into her briefcase.

"You will? That's all I was hoping for today, is a contact, someone impartial who would listen to our side of the story, finally. Because nobody has been willing to do that. Nobody. It's a sad case and the kids and my husband need help now. Here." I handed her a Christmas picture of the boys, Gerald and I. On the back, later hopefully, she would see the words, "The kids need your help." I walked away satisfied. Maybe too optimistic, I thought. Maybe nothing would come of it, but at least we had tried, again.

I was glad to see the sun when I got outside. It was quite a walk back to the car. Gerald was engrossed in a book and did not appear agitated that the forum lasted as long as it did. I described the event and let him know that it might prove productive since she had given me the name and number of someone to call.

"They all seemed like genuinely nice, helpful people. I'm glad I went." It was only noon, so we had plenty of time to take our drive toward an unknown southern Indiana town. We didn't know which one it would be, but we did know we wanted to find one and move there. We were tired of the city.

Gerald turned the radio station on WTLC and drove toward the expressway, while I slipped off my shoes, tilted the seat back and got comfortable.

CHAPTER 15

Two hours later, after lunch at a truck stop, we found the town of our dreams. As soon as we turned off the main road and traveled a few miles into the country, we entered a cozy, quiet town. We both liked it immediately and thought, this is it, this will be our next move.

"I'll bet this is the kind of town where you can leave your doors unlocked at night. I mean, I wouldn't, but I bet you could, huh Ger?"

"Yeah, probably. I like it." We were in total agreement. The more we roamed around town, the more we liked it. I spotted a community swimming pool and four tennis courts which certainly worked as selling items for me.

We cruised slowly up and down the streets looking for a house to rent, but found nothing. We jotted down a few real estate numbers so we could call later and see if there was anything in town.

The drive back home proved to be a little more exhausting but we left Sirlington in a cheery mood, firmly convinced that someday we would return and find a place to rent.

We rolled in at 10 P.M. Before going to sleep, I left our name and number on the message machine of several realtors. I told them to call us back if they had any apartments or houses available.

Early in the morning, I received a call from a Bernie Sessel. He mentioned that a beautiful, one-bedroom apartment was available, but unfortunately, it was located ten miles further south in a town we were not familiar with.

Gerald and I talked it over and decided we had better take what we could get down that way, since it was so difficult to find anything. We consented to see the apartment within a few days and if we liked it, we would move.

But I spent the morning feeling nervous about our hasty decisions. I thought about something I had learned, how people who have gone through crisis situations aren't supposed to make any more sudden major changes than necessary. And we weren't even through with our crisis yet.

After an hour or so of cartoons, Jonathan and Ginnylyn talked me into taking a walk. Jonathan hurried toward the railroad tracks. "I wanna go see a trains. C'mon guys." He waved at us to catch up with him.

"Wait a minute," I yelled. "You wait right there, Jon. I don't want you getting too close."

We sat on the grassy area and watched two trains clank by. It made Jonathan's day. As we leisurely walked home, I don't know what prompted me to take a different route, but I did. We had always followed the same way back before. This time, however, I zigzagged around and eventually cut through a vacant lot to get to the next street.

I couldn't believe it. I noticed an orange FOR RENT sign in the window of a small black and white house. I opened the metal gate, walked up to the front window and looked inside. Only the window to the enclosed front porch was left uncovered. All of the others were darkened with some large plastic garbage bags. I told the kids to follow me as I walked all around the house. I liked the fact that the lengthy, but narrow, front yard had a fence and some trees.

As the kids and I reached the back of the house, I realized it had to be a sign, because we were only a few steps away from Dad's garage. I had scouted all around the neighborhood and missed the house somehow.

My scheming brain cells began to race again. Now if it's just reasonable, I thought to myself. We could still save money by paying less rent and avoiding a phone and cable bill.

We walked our remaining twenty steps or so and opened the back gate to Dad's house. I rushed in to call and find out the amount of requested rent. For a mere two hundred and fifty dollars per month, Gerald and I could move in and give Dad his room back.

Gerald expressed the same sentiments when I called him, that he thought it might be best to wait awhile, until the time for a change felt more right. So we postponed our move to the country, but hung onto our plan to transfer to Sirlington some time in the future.

By the middle of June, we were all settled in. Though many things were inconvenient and aggravating at this time in our lives, the move certainly was much easier. A great deal of our possessions still remained in boxes, stored away. We only furnished the one bedroom house with enough to make us comfortable.

Gerald liked it. We called it our little cabin. A few days after scrubbing the dirty house clean, I rummaged around at garage sales to my heart's content. The best bargain I came across was a black and white television for ten dollars. Including a dining room rug, which I bought new, since I couldn't find what I was looking for, the total for interior decorating probably rounded out to about one hundred dollars.

We would be able to cut living expenses and have our own place to come home to again. And we would be able to save even more money since finally, after numerous applications and interviews, I had managed to obtain a steady, well paying nursing job at Whispering Pines Nursing Home. I had to dig through several boxes to find my white uniforms.

In essence, in the new place, we surrounded ourselves with what we needed to survive. The stove and refrigerator worked and water pressure was good. I jokingly said to Ger one morning, "Except for the T.V., Henry David Thoreau would be proud of us."

"Yeah, this will do. I'm still concerned about the neighborhood somewhat, all that broken glass back in the alley, even that one window of ours, not to mention the fact that your sister says there are gangs around here causing trouble all the time, but I guess we'll just have to make the best of it for a little longer." He propped up his pillows and sat up. "Neat lighting, huh, Karrol?" He referred to the way the sun twinkled through the thin, cheap bamboo blinds I had hung up across the front room window.

"Ooh, that is nice," I agreed. It felt great to know the sun was shining. "I am so glad summer is finally here."

"Me too," Gerald said as we stared some more at the special lighting effects which seemed to have a soothing affect on us both.

That day, after Gerald left for work, I decided to drive to Crestwood Edge to try and meet with Mrs. Smart, a lady that had spoken at the forum. We couldn't seem to connect by phone. It was one thing after another. She was off for a few days because her father had undergone some type of surgery. I procrastinated pursuing it for awhile due to the task of moving again. And now, apparently, Mrs. Smart could be found at the youth center everyday, but the phones weren't connected yet.

I stopped by the court house and asked for directions to the youth center. As I pulled into the parking lot, I saw several carpenters working on the entrance way. I asked if Mrs. Smart was inside and they said yes.

The scent of sawdust and fumes from the fresh paint were strong, but tolerable, I hoped. I walked past two offices and reached the last one. The door was open. She was sitting at her desk.

"Hello. Are you Jessica Smart?" She looked taller, different from the first time I saw her at the forum.

"Yes I am. Hello." She stood up to talk to me.

"Hi. I tracked you down finally. I'm Karrol Karlin. We finally get to talk to each other instead of leaving messages. She smiled and quickly set up a folding chair in front of her desk, but it was so dusty, she searched around until she found a rag, wiped the seat off, then placed a piece of newspaper on top of it.

"Yes. We weren't having any luck by phone, were we? I kept leaving messages with your friend, Lucy, I think it is, and with your sister. As you can see, they still need to do a few things so the center can open. We're almost there, but it just got too hectic running back and forth to both offices, so I decided at this point to just come here during the day, and they just hooked up the phones."

I explained again, my reasons for being there. I felt comfortable with her right away because she was so pleasant.

"I understand and I did read over your information. But let me first say, and I am sorry to have to tell you this, but we do have a problem. Just to let you know, I did keep calling you back, because I did not want to ignore you or have you feel I was being rude to you in any way, but I am an employee of the prosecutor's office and there's not really much I can do."

"Well, I thought there was a chance that the youth center would employ someone impartial who could check into our side of the story. I mean that is what the center is for, isn't it, to help kids in need?" Already I was feeling a sense of futility.

"That's correct. Now there are charges though, is that right?" she asked.

"Yes. They indicted him, but it was a totally one-sided investigation and they believed everything his ex-wife said in the medical records. Gerald never had a chance to defend himself. And nobody will look at the fact that these claims were filed with the police after a long family court fight. We had just managed to get visitation back with the kids. You know, like they said at the forum, about substantiation. I have the psychologist's report right here on my lap and she supports Gerald's innocence. Do you want to see it?" I offered the large brown envelope to her. I didn't want to stop talking because I knew the next thing out of her mouth again was going to be, "I can't help."

She was patient with me so I continued to explain that CPS was aware of our requests for help early on, prior to indictment. "The police, CPS, the prosecution, they were all informed by certified letters that there was a family court battle going on and a psychologist was evaluating the allegations. But none of them would listen. The saddest part about all this is the fact that they wouldn't wait on Dr. Cobers' evaluation."

I tried to give her as much information as possible. It was obvious she wasn't going to be able to help, but she was definitely there to help abused kids, if bureaucracy didn't stop her. I could sense her sincerity, even perhaps a desire to help in our case. But she was on the other side of the fence, for now.

I had to say one last thing. "They are wasting a great deal of taxpayer's money and ours and causing terrible emotional damage to us and our kids!"

She seemed overwhelmed by everything I had thrown at her. "I understand you've got a very bad situation here and if in fact your husband is innocent, then I certainly hope that in the end it is resolved in a way which honors the concepts of truth and justice. Maybe if the center was opened earlier, before charges, I could have checked into it and helped. It's sad and I'm sorry, whatever the situation, that it is happening. But technically, I really shouldn't even be talking with you. Like I said, we are here for the kids and I want to help, but at this point, in this case, at this time, my hands are tied. However, I wasn't going to ignore you or be rude since you contacted me with such a need for help."

She sounded so sincere, yet it was evident that I was at another dead end, unable to obtain the help our family so desperately needed. "Well, can I ask you this, then I won't take up anymore of your time. Do you think as the facts become known at the trial, if things don't go the mother's way, that people will finally see that the kids need help and finally do something? We are trying so hard to get some safeguards in place to protect them. One of our fears is that if the kids start telling the truth, that the abuse never happened, she may hurt them or run off to Mexico with Todd and Gerry. Then we'll never find them."

She paused for a moment, and seemed to be carefully choosing her words. "Well, I'm not an attorney, so I can't give advice, but maybe you could check into a court-appointed guardian with the court system that your husband filed for the custody or visitation. Maybe you can request an immediate hearing or something to secure the kids. Because I doubt police or CPS will do anything unless this turns in your favor." She added, "I do think it's admirable the way you are pursuing it if it happened as you said."

I realized she had over-extended herself. But before leaving I told her, "Maybe you can't help us now, but you might be seeing our kids one day. At least I got to see you. I saw the article about the youth center and your picture in the paper, and the forum was great. By the way, I'm still waiting to hear from a Leslie Lassiter, from downstate, maybe they can do something.

128

I'll let you know what happens. Anyway, thanks for your time."
We shook hands and I left.

I refrained from crying for a change because at least someone wasn't abrupt, rude and indifferent to my cries for help and justice.

Mrs. Smart also mentioned legal aid when I told her that Gerald and I couldn't afford any more legal fees, unless we could pay monthly. So on the way home, I stopped at the library and called but reached a recording. There were certain times and I would just have to show up and sign in.

I thought I'd try one more thing first. There was still the lawyer in Kellton who I had not been successful in talking too yet.

When I got home, I explained to Dad I would be up in the bedroom making some phone calls. I grabbed the phonebook and cordless telephone. Tiger was sleeping as usual, so I gave him a few strokes before I sat down on the bed.

I discovered two important things after a few calls. Legal aid did not handle felonies and two different lawyers said the same thing, that a court-appointed guardian often made things worse in a situation like this, rather than helped. I didn't understand why, but their advice was enough to stir me away from the idea.

The nightmarish tenseness returned. My stomach knotted up and a headache began to throb. It hurt to think that Todd and Gerry were spending day after day being told that their dad hurt them and abandoned them. They probably had no idea about our long struggle to get them back. All they needed was the truth, that their dad loved them. That was at the root of all of their aches and pains, along with the other adverse side effects of a mother's betrayal.

The usual multitude of preoccupying thoughts and fears resurfaced and began to haunt me. What would happen if he received a guilty verdict? Then what? Our lives destroyed, it would in turn affect so many other family members and friends.

So often I had tried to remain upbeat and hopeful about the unfortunate matters at hand. When things got me down, Ger was there and picked me up. When he was down, emotionally, feeling like it was all so hopeless, I tried to help. Sometimes it worked, sometimes it didn't, like one particular day when he really started questioning where God was during all of our turmoil. I reassured him that God wasn't responsible for all of the misery, the unfairness, that in fact, God would be responsible for righting things in the end. He sarcastically responded, "Yeah sure. We'll see, won't we?"

After getting nowhere again, the ultimate fear of losing everything seemed more like a possible reality. I could only hope and pray that in the end we would be able to turn this thing around.

As far as winning in the case of seeing the boys, if I never got to see their sweet faces again, it would be all right, as long as I knew they were aware of the truth and they were happy, healthy, and safe.

I knew Gerald felt the same, he said so once.

That night I didn't say a word to Gerald because I was not going to ruin our evening. We stopped by to visit Lucy and Sanford for a while, then spent the most relaxing, enjoyable time together at the Owl Theatre in Freeland, one of the last old-fashioned theatres left in America. The Owl's refreshments are cheap and for the last twenty years, the admission price has amazingly remained at three dollars and fifty cents. But the quaint theatre's most unique features include a cartoon prior to show time, like there's supposed to be, and a ten-minute half-time intermission that enables patrons to line up and take advantage of free coffee, punch, and homemade cookies and strudel. We were captivated by the incredibly poignant and entertaining movie, Guarding Tess.

I worked hard at learning my new job, especially all of the resident's names. Erin, my partner in the evenings, and I made a good team. Things ran smoothly for the most part, even when we had to handle various emergencies. It sure felt good to be utilizing more of my nursing skills again and contributing more financially.

Gerald encountered more stress when the company he worked for merged, which meant he had to travel an extra hour each day to and from work in city traffic. We both knew it would begin to feel like too much of a burden and he would have to look for something closer.

He made the decision to wait until January to begin paramedic classes, and hoped everything would be cleared up by then. It was his dream, to become a paramedic. And I was all for dreams coming true, happy dreams anyway.

Dad tagged along as we took another trip down south to see our little town. He saw the beauty and experienced the peaceful feeling which the country atmosphere provided. In fact, he encouraged us. "I hope you find a place down here and stay put for the rest of your life."

Before leaving Sirlington, we picked up a couple of area newspapers. We came up with the idea that if Gerald had to switch jobs, maybe he could find something down south where we planned to settle down in the near future. He would check with local hospitals and ambulance services first.

Unfortunately, I was just beginning to feel comfortable with my new job. But if I could find a good job too, I was still eager to make the transition.

We worried constantly about our car windows at night. With summertime and the kids out of school, the neighborhood seemed even more wild and threatening. A certain group of kids continually strutted down the alleyway smashing windows just for kicks. We decided not to waste the landlord's money and simply boarded up the back windows.

Katie had a confrontation with them all one day when they showed up while she was in the backyard. I worried that it might make things worse for her and dad, that they might come back and really cause trouble, since she had pleaded with them to find something constructive to do with their time.

I didn't tell Gerald about the gun incident. I knew he would want to check us right into a motel, and we were uprooted enough, as far as I was concerned. I just put the baseball bat in between the refrigerator and the wall and decided to defend myself if anyone came looking for trouble. The pistol that a mean-looking kid had pointed directly at me one day as I sat on the picnic bench in Dad's back yard, turned out to be a B.B. gun, but it still scared the life out of me. So needless to say, I was on guard, and had no qualms about leaving as soon as the time felt right. Gerald began to worry more and more about my safety when he was gone for such long hours or night shifts. I could see the pressure building up.

We pushed ourselves to attend my godson's graduation, since I did not want to miss it, but both of us were feeling so lost and worn out. Again, our friends offered their continued support. But on the way home, Gerald drove right past the Indiana state line into Illinois and picked up two six-packs of beer. Before entering the liquor store, he lamented, "You know it's been over a year now, since I've seen the boys. I probably won't even get to see my kids graduate. I'll be rotting in some prison somewhere."

I didn't say a word, only inhaled and let out a good long sigh. I was tired of trying to say or do something positive whenever the next negative aspect hit us, and I figured if Ger was determined to drink, then he was going to drink.

The next day though, I offered to find him a room to rent if he was going to continue. Luckily he came to his senses and took it upon himself to obtain a prescription for Antabuse. He said he planned to make the AA meeting downtown at the church too, on Wednesday evening. Wednesday came and he kept his word.

Rennie and Bonnie held their annual 4th of July picnic at their house in the backyard. Although it was comforting to be around family, I couldn't help thinking about the fact that it was the day when Americans cherish the idea of a free heart and mind, and recognize a sense of pride in their country. Whereas, I wondered if Ger and I could ever feel the joy of freedom again.

We left early to make sure we were home by dark. For the past two weeks, it seemed like the supply of firecrackers to the kids in the neighborhood was endless. Even though it was incredibly noisy compared to our old neighborhood on the Fourth, we realized that it was a day of celebration and the festive spirit of the night prompted us to sit out on the lawn chairs and admire the sky as it lit up. A park nearby supplied the annual fireworks display. I had forgotten we lived so close.

Gerald mentioned Todd and Gerry, how he missed them earlier today at Rennie's and how he hoped they weren't getting into some mischief, playing with cherry bombs or something like that.

"Remember when we did all those sparklers at Rennie's with 'em, and the snakes. Todd was infatuated with the snakes as we lit them over at the playground," I reminisced.

"Yeah, I remember," Gerald answered. "Was that the year Rennie set up the croquet set and we taught 'em how to play croquet?" he asked.

"Yeah, and they would hit the ball so hard. We couldn't get them to hit it easier so they could line up in front of the wicket." We both laughed. I began to rub the back of my neck. I was tired of looking upward, but knew the finale was coming and wanted to see it. So I looked up again.

"I wonder if they're involved in any sports. I hope they're getting to play baseball or something. I really miss going to their games. I know you miss that too, coaching and everything. Hey, remember the way all the kids used to throw their bats? I thought for sure somebody was going to get clobbered." We laughed again as we pictured it. Todd and Gerry were no exceptions, they threw their bats too. "Oh, and the way all the kids loved it when Todd and Gerry showed up because they knew they would hit home runs."

"Yeah, I remember. I remember everything. God I hope they're not getting into trouble tonight. You know how Todd likes to experiment with everything. Damn Karrol, I feel so helpless. I've lost my sons man, and can't seen to do a damn thing about it. " He suddenly got quiet, so I knew it was time to revert back to the present and just try and enjoy the rest of the fireworks.

"This is it, the finale, here it comes." I plugged my ears to subdue the loud explosive booms. We both remarked how beautiful the colors were. A few minutes later, the sky got dark again, and we went inside.

CHAPTER 16

"**K**arrol, what's the matter?" Katie asked as she came downstairs and saw me sitting on the couch crying. I explained that I had used the telephone to make a couple of calls.

"Oh everything, that's all. Our car windshield got shattered last night, on Gerald's way to work. He could have been killed." I sniffled and wiped my nose with a tissue.

"Oh my God, what happened, where was he, somewhere here in the neighborhood or...?" she asked.

"No, no, on the expressway, a piece of metal or something from a truck," I explained. "You should see it, there's a whole on the passenger's side the size of a basketball. I just saw the other day how a guy did get killed by the same thing that happened to him. I saw it on the news. Our windshield looks just like his did, except Ger was lucky. It hit the passenger's side."

"So he's all right then? But your car's messed up now, huh?" she asked.

"Yeah. But that's not the half of it." I hinted that there were other reasons for my being so upset. I explained that our good lawyer had withdrawn and we finally obtained a court-appointed one, but there was another continuance. "Now we have to wait until February. Can you believe it, not until February. We want to get this over with so much." She was shocked when I let her know about the delay.

Then I told her how I had just gotten off the phone with the lady from downstate, the one who was supposed to help. "They all say the same thing, they can't do anything because of the charges."

"They won't even read that psychologist's report?"

"Nope, nothing. Nobody will do a darn thing to help us. In the meantime, we can't do anything about Todd and Gerry. It's never ending. I can't stand it," I confessed. "It feels like cancer of the spirit, Katie, really, that's what it's like. It just keeps eating away at us."

She sat close and tried to comfort me. She encouraged me to hang in there, and said that the truth would come out at the trial, then we could all get help. But I wasn't budging. I felt miserable and decided to stay that way for the time being.

"Yeah, and what if they don't listen to the truth and twist everything around, you know the way they do. I'm telling you, if Ger's found guilty, it's all over, that's it." I took a few deep breaths and wiped the tears rolling down my cheeks.

"What do you mean by that, Karrol? You're scaring me. What do you mean?" She pleaded for an answer.

I dramatized my feelings some more. "It's all over, that's all, no more fighting, the bad guys win. That's what I mean. Don't you get it, sometimes the bad guys win."

Katie was obviously alarmed by my comments and knew there was cause to worry, that finally things were getting the best of me.

She tried her best to get me to settle down, but I was in no mood to hear it. I jumped up and said, "Bye, thanks for listening, but I've gotta go."

I cut through the back yard, went across the alley and unlocked my front door, so I could get my bike. Bicycling had become a hobby again for the summertime. I pedaled quickly over to a nearby park, leaned my bike against a tree and sat on a hard bench.

Every time we turned around, I thought, something was being thrown at us to make things worse. And what good are forums, what good is all the talk and all their great plans, if nobody can step in and do anything when people desperately cry out for help, I wondered. With all of the extra praying I was doing, it seemed as if it was useless. Instead of receiving strength from God, I felt abandoned. It wasn't fair, the way we kept getting sabotaged, as if someone or something was bound and determined to force us to lose, to just give up.

Usually, I'd recover and try, try again. This time, with so many other stresses going on, I wondered where the strength or desire to keep on trying, for nothing, would come from.

My father's deteriorating health, especially, was another serious concern. He kept complaining about a pain in his chest area, but his doctor couldn't determine the reason for it. The restless days passed, while the nights in the neighborhood continued to be noisy and feel unsafe. On pure instinct one day, I decided to drive south once again to Sirlington to see if I could get lucky and find a house for rent.

While I sat in the corner restaurant on the main highway, a short distance from the town, I overheard a gentleman say that his sister had a place for rent. I seized the moment and asked if I could see it. He said, "Sure. Go contact my sister at the welfare office." He wrote down Karrolyn's name and where I needed to go. She was a friendly, energetic person and, luckily, agreed to take us on as tenants.

We decided to make our move, literally, on August first. I saw a few job possibilities in the local paper and knew with a hospital being close by, Gerald and I could probably find work. The other choice made no sense. Why sit around and worry about burglary, or someone slashing our tires, or smashing our windows out, like my sister's car? She was fed up too. But Dad was a hard one to sell on the idea of moving. Nothing seemed to bother him about the neighborhood.

Gerald and I both agreed that it didn't feel right, putting our life on hold until we reached the end of our nightmare. Mainly because, it seemed never ending.

The only thing that didn't feel right about our chance for a new beginning, was leaving when Dad needed more help. But we couldn't stand it anymore. We needed a positive change.

Our new home only had two bedrooms and was rather small, which made it necessary to utilize a storage unit for the rest of our belongings. Boxes were unpacked, again. And the walls began to look like home as familiar pictures and paintings were hung. Of course, the stress caused by another move caught up with us, but we soon realized it was worth it.

We had finally left the city behind. When we glanced out of the living room window toward the backyard, we witnessed the country scene we had been hoping for. The yard stretched on and on. There was so much open space and it was incredibly quiet. The bright stars at night were a source of inspiration to us.

The paneled kitchen and living room walls made it feel like another country cabin. The only thing missing was a fireplace. We had to adjust, going to sleep listening to crickets chirping instead of the constant clanking of the trains two blocks from our last location.

We had escaped at least some of the tension, some of our fears. However, one fear relentlessly continued to occupy my thoughts, and it was something other than a guilty verdict for Gerald.

Dad stopped eating, lost weight, and could hardly walk again. His cherished quality of life, although already somewhat limited, began to rapidly slip away. After many trips to the doctor and the emergency room, we no longer had to deal with the unknown, only an insidious killer called cancer.

I quickly realized how tragically cancer destroys a life. The disease shows no mercy to the victim or loved ones who try to help. Everyone suffers so much pain. The crisis pulled our family apart for awhile. More amazingly, though, the crisis managed also to bring us together, especially in a joint effort to fight for Dad's last wishes, well actually, his last orders.

One day while visiting him in the hospital, he felt strong enough to sit up in the wheelchair. I rolled him over to a window so he could see outside, since he had been confined for weeks. He loved the outdoors.

I suddenly realized that he had gotten up because he was under the impression that he was finally going home. But the doctors had warned us that it wasn't possible yet, that he would die in a matter of hours, seventy-two at the most. In essence, it was up to me to break the news as gently as I could.

Oddly enough, he had been so patient and followed doctor's orders, but I knew very well that he would not want to hear about any more stalling.

He informed me, "I'll tell you one damn thing, I'm going home again before I die!" His lips puckered a little, and he gave me a stern, unwavering look. But his eyes softened as I replied, "I know Dad. I know. We'll get you home. We promise." He saw my tears and we hugged.

138

Finally Dad came home. The hospital bed and oxygen were the only things different. Mostly he saw family photos on the walls and listened to his familiar television programs. We kept the television tuned into westerns or wildlife shows. He heard country western music and the pestering but welcomed cries of his grandchildren. When the kids weren't fighting though, they both tried to be a big help, and handed their Pocka whatever he asked for.

Dad also sat up in his favorite chair and knew in his final days that he was greatly loved. The lonely, sterile, artificially lit hospital ward, the death row of many cancer-stricken patients, where everything must have seemed bleak, unfamiliar and lifeless, was left behind. He had escaped.

We were so lucky to be able to spend quality time with him and say our good-byes. Fighter that he was, he marched along so bravely. Then he weakened physically, hour by hour, until only inhaling and exhaling took place.

That's when I told him. "You rest now, Dad. It's okay. You can go to sleep now, whenever you want to. You're home, Dad. You've been so brave and you are such a loving father. We'll all miss you so much, Dad. I love you so much. But you rest now." I held his hand up to my lips and kissed it.

He somehow mustered up enough energy to respond. "Okay," he whispered, and we continued to hold hands.

Before I left for home that night, I hugged him and said good-bye four times. I knew it would be the last time I'd see my father alive. My sister called a few hours later to let Gerald and I know that Dad's suffering was finally over.

On November 21, 1994, my father took his final respiration after his short, but incredibly brave bout with lung cancer. He died at home where he belonged, hospice style. Our hearts ached like never before, but the whole family felt good about one thing, we had fought to give Dad his last wish and we had succeeded.

There was even more agonizing pain to deal with the day of Dad's funeral. Our incredible bad luck regarding car trouble continued. While I was inside the funeral home, experiencing one of the saddest days of my life, someone had run into our car.

It was a hit and run. It was not drivable. We knew it would cost us at least five hundred dollars to fix it, money which, of course, we did not have, especially right before Christmas.

We did what we had to that day, paid our last tribute to Dad, along with other family and friends, then rushed home in Dad's multi-dented white Chevy to check on Tiger. His health had deteriorated in the last few days. In fact, before they closed my father's casket, I placed two pictures of my dog inside.

Gerald and I wondered if he'd still be alive. He couldn't walk any more and was more confused. I wanted to end his suffering, but thought it would be too much to come home to his absence directly after saying farewell to Dad.

We tended to him gently and lovingly as he laid on top of an exercise mat with a pillow under his head, until the next evening. After several phone calls and gruesome anticipation, a kind veterinarian called back and offered to help.

I snuggled up to Tiger and he looked at me with his sweet brown, tired eyes. The cold, dark, lonely night chilled us as we moved him carefully to the car.

The vet was so caring, there for us right when we needed his help. As suspected, there was nothing more to be done. Old age and finally congestive heart failure had gotten the best of my old pal.

We told him what a great friend he had been and how much we loved him. Gerald and I both shed tears as we held Tiger's head and said good-bye as the vet injected him with the potent shot which would end his suffering.

On the ride home, Ger tried to be comforting, but of course, both of us were experiencing too much pain all at once. We felt overwhelmed by our hard times.

CHAPTER 17

The holidays zoomed by and were difficult since two precious family members, Dad and Tiger, were no longer with us. But I remembered how my father always said, "Life goes on," so I tried to hang onto the hope that the pain would lessen and joy would be an emotion I could feel again someday.

Our Christmas puppy, Angel, helped to liven up the house again. Of course she began to get on our nerves as we learned that her favorite things to chew were pillow cases, shoes, and the remote control.

On January 13th, the pre-trial went smoothly and quickly. Neither side had anything new. But when it came time for the depositions prior to the February 6th scheduled trial, it was a different story.

"I'll bet you money, it will be cancelled at the last minute or something and nobody bothers to tell us," I wagered. I spoke from the viewpoint of experience. We had already received one note in the mail informing Gerald of how he had failed to show up for an appearance. We wrote back and explained that we would have been there, if we had known about it. Gerald's court-appointed lawyer apparently didn't know anything about it either.

The anticipation of seeing Todd and Gerry at the January 19th hearing caused me to toss and turn for several nights. I hoped and prayed that they would give us some sign of hope that they were not totally lost to the falsehood which was managing to destroy what father and sons once had, mainly love and trust.

Gerald cautioned me as we rode toward the court house. "Now really, Karrol, I'm afraid if you say anything to the boys it may jeopardize my case, so please try to refrain, okay?"

"I can blow the kids a kiss, at least, can't I, if I get the chance?" I pleaded. "You wouldn't let me pursue the T-shirt idea." I had planned to buy T-shirts which spelled out clearly, in bold colors, We love you, Todd and Gerry. Gerald growled at my idea of blowing the kids a kiss, but he didn't say no, so I figured the first opportunity I got and managed eye contact, I'd do just that.

We parked, stepped out of the car, grabbed hands and proceeded to the entrance. After passing through security, we walked upstairs like we always did. Half way up the stairs, I looked to the left and there they were, Gerald's long lost sons. Todd fidgeted as usual as he stood next to Gerry and Flora while they sat in chairs. I paused on the steps and said, "There they are, hon. There they are. They don't look that much bigger, look." Gerald glanced quickly, then nudged me to keep moving.

Then the crushing blow to the heart hit. Only Flora looked up. It was as if the kids were robots and she had total control. I expressed my sadness to Gerald and he explained, "They're just doing what they have to, honey, they're restrained by their mother. They have to do whatever she says."

I don't know what I had been thinking or praying for. I should have known better, I finally realized. It became clear to me at that moment, that the boys had indeed done what they were good at, adapted. They had moved on with their lives. Dad and Karrol were no longer a part of it. It appeared that we had painfully lost the bond which we had all once shared as a family.

I felt sick. I wanted to give up. Fighting did not seem important anymore. I could not tell how Gerald felt, because he just kept plugging along, and proceeded to follow through with the purpose for coming, the depositions.

Mr. Ranski, our lawyer, showed up on time. We were grateful for that. He said a few words to Gerald, then headed for the prosecutor's office. We sat and waited downstairs, since he said the depositions would probably take place there.

I noticed the kids and Flora were sitting in the prosecutor's office. At one point, Todd stood up and walked toward the doorway, but I heard something, then he sat back down.

Ranski walked back out and passed right by us as he saw the deputy prosecutor, a tall, slim, blond-haired woman. They stood about six feet away, when I heard her say, "Hello, Mr. Ranski. Well, we have two problems. First of all, the boys are sick. I mean you can go ahead with the deposition if you want, but they're sick. They haven't been in school all week and one of them even threw up on himself on the way over here. And the other thing is, he can't be in the room, because of the restraining order." She nodded her head in Gerald's direction as she informed Ranski.

Gerald and I knew something would not go as planned, as usual. Now we knew what. It was obvious that Gerald felt exasperated. He had asked our lawyer if the convenient restraining order, which had been thrust upon him for no good reason, would create a problem and prevent him from being able to attend the depositions. Ranski explained that as far as he knew, Gerald had a right to face his accusers.

Our only attempts at contacting the kids were by sending them birthday and Christmas cards. I had made that one phone call to the kids, right after we were informed of the claims, just to tell them that we loved them and would see them when we could.

Gerald expressed his frustration to Ranski. "But I thought I asked you about this the other day, to make sure I could be here."

"Well, I thought you could, that the restraining order didn't hold for the depositions," Ranski answered. "But she says you can't be here. So we can do one or the other, wait and try and see if the judge will let you be here for them, or go ahead today. And she says the kids are sick too."

"Yeah well, the thing you need to know, Walter, is that somebody's always sick when there is a court date or a doctor's appointment involved. Either that or it's car trouble and she doesn't show up. So frankly, I'm surprised that she's even here today."

I immediately thought about the trial being continued again due to the setback. "Did you see those kids? They are so lost, they can't even look at their dad." I stood up and started to cry. "Lost because a biased, incompetent system wouldn't pay attention to the truth!" I ran toward the door and yelled back to Gerald, "I'll be waiting in the car."

When I reached the car, I realized I didn't have any keys. As I tilted my head back and leaned against the car, misty drops of snow began to hit my face. I asked God what we did to deserve such punishment, such overwhelming pain. I cried some more and thought about how Gerald, once again, was handling the ugly realities of the day, so much better than I. Gerald was so sweet and understanding when he returned. Yet it should have been me comforting him.

We sat in the car with the heat on. Finally the kids walked out. They had colorful jackets on. They were quite a distance away. I said my quiet good-byes to them that day and wished not for a reunion, like I used to, only for them to know the truth, that their father loved them and never hurt them.

Ger stared at the kids and said, "This hurts Karrol, the distance. We used to be so close. But hey, at least we know they're still alive and living in the country." Men let go of things so much easier. I couldn't decide if this was a blessing or a curse.

The delay wasn't as bad as we thought. Depositions would be taken January 30th and the trial, supposedly, would only be postponed a week or so. We hoped that it would be the end of the continuances. Gerald had purposely not booked any work for a couple of weeks, for the week of the trial and one week following. I would have to utilize sick time and I hated taking off work. Gerald wanted to be working more and making money, but it was difficult to schedule and reschedule so often due to the court dates.

Toward the end of January, as planned, Ger began to work on his dream of becoming a paramedic. He had mixed emotions about beginning the classes, because he had hoped that his troubles would be over.

He acted very disturbed the day he came home after the depositions were held. As assumed, he was not allowed to be in the room with the kids, or Flora, his accusers. I came home from work for lunch to see what had occurred.

"Go ahead and eat and then I'll give you the news," Ger said calmly, though he appeared very agitated.

"Oh boy. Okay, let me get a sandwich." I opened the refrigerator door. Angel came over and started jumping up on my leg and begging for something to eat. I fixed her a sandwich too. She obeyed the command of 'sit' in order to be rewarded.

144

I washed down my sandwich with a Diet Pepsi. "Okay, let me have it."

"Well, here's what Ranski said. Are you ready? Because here's how he put it to me. He said that if he hadn't met me and heard my side of the story and known the circumstances, he'd believe the kids. He said sure, there are some inconsistencies, but they sound plausible. He also said it's going to be real tough to win my case if Todd and Gerry get up on the stand and start crying or show a lot of emotion because the jury will feel sorry for them."

"God, I don't believe this! This is so unreal. It's so sickening, you know?"

"Yeah. I guess, like you said, the kids are lost. You know what else he told me?"

"What?" I asked.

He said that prosecutor, or deputy prosecutor, whatever she is, was almost in tears. And that's probably why they gave her this case, because they know she's the emotional type. I asked him, how she could be so naive, and why she refused to wait on Dr. Cobers' report."

"Oh brother. Well, so much for objectivity, huh? Well, we knew from the other day that the kids were probably pretty lost, didn't we? It's just gonna be up to our lawyer to educate the jury on how this kind of thing happens, and Dr. Cobers. Like all those articles on how parents use this in divorce cases and how the kids begin to believe the abuse is real, you know those syndromes we read about." I glanced at the kitchen clock.

"Yeah, if Ranski and Dr. Cobers can convince them. I'm not so sure they can, or that the jurors will listen, especially if they see the kids crying and saying I did this to them."

"It will work out, hon, the truth just has to prevail."

Gerald began to raise his voice and nothing but doubts seemed to be conveyed as he spoke. I could tell he was feeling as if the situation was hopeless again. "You know, Karrol, that justice stuff is all fine and good, talk wise. I mean, sure, it sounds good but the reality is, it's not the way it works sometimes. And besides, you don't know what I know." He squinted his eyes in a furtive way.

"What don't I know, what happened today? Tell me, Ger."
He still looked distant, not connected, and it scared me.

Then he told me all about how the prosecution had offered
him a deal, two counts of Class D Misdemeanors, he thought
Ranski said, sentence suspended, probation, maybe some
counseling and best of all, the sexual abuse aspect of the charges
would be dropped. It was obvious that he was considering it
since he no longer believed in the justice system prevailing in his
favor.

"Oh great. And how does that solve anything? How does
that help you get your life back? You know what all the research
says, don't take any deals." I began lecturing. I looked at the
clock again, stood up and hastily put my coat on, letting him
know I didn't want to hear any more about deals. "I think you
had better rethink this, Ger, and quit listening to their scare
tactics."

"Well, you're not the one going to prison, I am. Are you
saying I shouldn't consider this? Because I'm not so sure.
Look, they're going to try and crucify me, Karrol with my
alcoholism history and Todd and Gerry saying I did it." He
reached for his pack of cigarettes.

I sat back down. I tried to let him know that I was listening
to his concerns. And I had to confess, "No, honey, I can't say
what you should do or shouldn't do. If they made you some kind
of deal, then only you can choose yes or no."

"That's right," he said defiantly as he began to light his
cigarette.

"But think about it for a minute. What are they doing
offering you a deal without any jail time? I mean how does that
serve any justice? They went through all of this, just to let an
alleged child molester go free? Maybe this is a good sign.
Maybe they finally see how foolish they're going to look in that
courtroom, once we get the facts out. Don't you see? By
offering you this, they just want to assure a conviction of guilty,
because face the trial, and they've got a good chance of losing."

I took a long deep breath. "And maybe our justice system is
too screwed up to make any sense, to give anybody back the
justice victimized people deserve. But I do know if we don't try

and fight this all the way, then they win and you and the kids will lose. After all, it's just another form of abuse. Somebody's got to expose it, or it will just keep on destroying our lives and probably a lot of other families."

He listened but did not let go of his skepticism. "Yeah, yeah, yeah. More of your optimistic, philosophical mumbo jumbo. We'll see, Karrol. We'll just see what happens here." He noticed I was already late for work. "You better go." He puffed nervously on his cigarette, as I walked out the door.

Later in the evening, Gerald informed me that he would not plea bargain because he did not want to admit to something which he had never done. He said, "That's what clinched it, the fact that I would have to sign something saying I did things which never happened. Remember, I'm innocent. I did not do anything wrong. She is the one totally messing up the kid's lives. Just when are they going to hold her accountable for all of the damage she's done?" He paused and then smiled at me. "So mark that on your calendar. And I guess we'll go try and fight this thing. Whatever we have to do to survive this, let's do it."

I let him know I was thoroughly pleased and proud of him and his new outlook. We had been through so much. I didn't want him to give up. But what if he was right, I secretly asked myself. What if his willingness to see it through, his continued fight for justice ends up costing him his freedom? We want our freedom back and our kids. My thoughts began to race again. I came to the conclusion that it was up to God again and the intelligence and goodness of certain key people to see us through our nightmare.

After a simple dinner of meat loaf and scalloped potatoes, we sat close to each other on the couch and watched a rerun of "Who's the Boss" and the silly "Married with Children." Then Gerald moved to the kitchen table and began to read his Anatomy and Physiology book until Karley, his eldest daughter, called from Washington. Gerald let her know the trial was set for February 27th.

"Tell her I wish she could be here sitting next to me," I said. Gerald relayed the message.

We called it a night after watching the news. The world sure has its problems, I thought, after hearing more about the earthquakes in Japan, the avalanches in India, shootings, killings everywhere, every day of the year, it seemed. Then of course, we were inundated with more of the heart-breaking Simpson story.

I woke up the next morning in a good mood for a change, remembering a dream which involved the boys. In the dream, Todd and Gerry came walking toward me. We sat down on a bench at some sort of mall. At first they were frowning, but as we started talking, everything seemed all right. They smiled. We joked around and it felt like old times. We were having fun again. Then Todd whispered in my ear, "I still want to live with you and Dad, but Mom says I can't because of the sexual abuse."

I told him, "Don't worry, Todd, Gerry, everything will be all right. Your dad loves you guys. Gerry, Todd, you guys just remember that, okay? Let's hear it."

"We love you, Dad," they said in unison loudly, then giggled.

But with each passing day and night, as February moved along and the date of the trial became more of a reality, both Gerald and I began to react to the heightening stressful event.

Ger caught another cold. He tried his best to concentrate on his paramedic studies. Usually he came home from class feeling inspired and upbeat. But not on February 8th. He did something totally out of character and began to talk about his case. He remained aggravated because Ranski hadn't returned any of his calls, although he had sent us the depositions, so we could review them. Gerald wanted to meet with him to discuss the children's latest comments and some strategies for his trial. However, Gerald kept leaving messages, but Mr. Ranski would not return his calls.

"I'm telling you, Karrol, I tried tonight, but I couldn't stay focused. This thing is really starting to affect me. I mean, we're supposed to be sitting down and working on my case, right, on how to prove the truth?"

He got up, walked to the kitchen and filled the coffee pot halfway with water.

"I know," I agreed. "We're running out of time now and there's so much we don't know, huh? We don't know what witnesses he's going to call or if he has even sent out any subpoenas yet or taken depositions like we asked." I sat in the brown chair across from him while he returned to the couch and sat down.

"Yeah, and this thing with the kids saying it happened. It's making me sick, Karrol. When they know it never happened. Their mother, yeah, maybe she's sick enough to believe it or something because she wants it to be true, but the boys, they know what we did when we were together."

I hated to remind him, but I had to. "Well, I'm sorry, honey, but I'm not so sure. Remember that one article that talked about Piaget's work, the one that said until about age eleven, kids have trouble differentiating reality from other stuff, dreams and thoughts. If someone keeps telling 'em over and over again that something happened and they talk about it like it's real, then, at some point, it probably becomes a real memory to them. I'm sorry, I know it's so unbelievable, but that's what they say happens."

Gerald remained angry and upset as we discussed the purpose for seeing another lawyer on Saturday. He threatened to sue somebody, anybody, so that people would think twice about putting any other innocent people through such a terrible ordeal, and messing up any other kids.

"Well, that's what I want to ask this new lawyer, how to pursue things afterwards, if maybe we can sue on behalf of the kids. Of course, we need some other vital tips since Ranski's not providing us with much." I spoke softly, hoping that Gerald might settle down and lower his voice.

But instead, he jumped up and walked over to the bookshelf. He grabbed his AA book. "That prosecutor, the way they indicted me. They wouldn't wait on Dr. Cobers' report. Here it is, I'll show you what they've done." He quoted Herbert Spencer, 'There is a principle which is a bar against all information, which is proof against all arguments and which cannot fail to keep a man in everlasting ignorance, that principle is contempt prior to investigation'." He slammed the book shut and set it back up on the shelf.

"I know. I know, sweetheart, it's all been so unfair. There ought to be a law, really, a law that says mediation has to take place right away, that they have to step in and be willing to do an impartial investigation when this happens in cases where a custody or visitation fight is going on." I offered my support.

He finally lowered his voice, but sounded so hurt as he said, "That's what really gets to me, their little one-sided investigation and refusing to wait on Dr. Cobers' report. Why did it have to be like this?" he asked.

I certainly had no answers for him.

The next evening we were back to trying to forget it all again, for a while. We played cards, then later challenged each other to a game of Scrabble. It had been a long time since we had done anything like that.

We were determined to carry on with our lives. Yet we knew the next eighteen days would be our last chance to hope, pray and try to do something which would make us feel more secure about the trial.

Fortunately, we did find the time to review the depositions before seeing the lawyer in Kellton. Gerald and I both expressed the same sentiments. We didn't see anything so threatening. In fact, we found a great deal of material that we thought might help to defend Gerald.

"Here Ger, take a look at this list, the chronological order of events. I'll give one to the new lawyer today along with some other stuff." I handed him the yellow sheet of paper.

"Oh good, okay." He sat down at the kitchen table and began to read. The long list of dates began with February 7th, 1992 and ended with the upcoming trial date of February 27th, 1995.

The ride to Kellton lasted about an hour and a half, but it wasn't as bad as we thought it would be. We parked at one of the underground parking lots. The wind chilled us right to the bone as we walked about a fourth of a mile to the high rise office building. An elderly elevator operator welcomed us inside and directed us to the right floor.

We located the office door and walked in. I could tell it was a Saturday because it was so quiet. We were the only ones around, except for one receptionist. Gerald and I began to read while we waited.

I found an interesting book lying on the table in front of me which dealt with divorce cases. I scanned through it, then noticed an excerpt in a newspaper about a shocking case about a father who had finally regained visitation with his daughter. When he and his fiancée went to pick up his daughter, his ex-wife killed them both. I thought about the horror stories of domestic fatalities and knew that more often it was a woman who ended up dead.

Finally a gentleman came out and escorted us into his office. We spent an intense two hours with him. He explained that the prosecution couldn't try their whole case and convict on just medical records.

"Well, that's just about what they're trying to do, the records, depositions and the kids saying that it happened. Yet, here you have the poor kids denying it for so long, Todd defending his father in Dr. Cobers' office, finally giving in to his mother and saying it happened once. Then the next thing you know, Todd's certain that the abuse happened throughout an entire year. And not only that, but with the help of the prosecutors and his mother, according to where they lived and what school and which grade he was in, they even determined the time period in which it all supposedly happened. There's only one major problem. The bunk beds that he always mentioned, we didn't even own them at the time. We bought them a year and a half after he says the abuse began or eight months after he says the abuse ended, depending upon which way people prefer to look at the evidence." I hurried and added, "And there's one more thing. My sister lived with us from April through July of 1991, because she had just had her son, and there are several pictures at the time which show the crib and bed we had at the time. There were no bunk beds." I felt like shaking the issue into somebody's brain.

The lawyer, even Gerald, looked dumbfounded. "And what about the time period for the other son?" the lawyer asked.

"Well, little Gerry's the one that says Todd's lying right next to him," I explained.

"That's what's so incredible," Gerald interjected. "Here my sons are the prosecution's key witnesses to say I did this to them, and yet the boys often talk about being in the same room, Gerry says at the same time, with the bunk beds, but neither one of them ever saw it happen. In Dr. Cobers' report, she mentions how the boys always say they know it happened. But the prosecution's key witnesses to the crime, the victims themselves, never once saw it happen." Gerald sighed and decided he had said enough about the one issue.

The lawyer said, "Well that is pretty incredible. Let me ask you, do they have any physical evidence?"

"No," Gerald explained. "See, the kids always had a problem with loose stools, Flora even says that. But the same doctor the prosecution wants to bring in as their key witness about the physical evidence part said his findings were NOT, and I forget the medical word, but it meant something like synonymous. In other words, what he found as he examined the boys, he said, did not indicate or support that sexual abuse had happened. And that same doctor says there can be other reasons for the diarrhea problem. He seemed concerned, sure, but because of what Flora was telling him, all the bull shit."

I interjected an important point. "Not only that, but she told the police lacerations were found. The police wrote it down and the doctor said no. She mentioned another doctor to CPS who supposedly found evidence. We tracked him down too. You know what Gerry had? Food poisoning."

The lawyer shook his head in disbelief. He urged us to provide the jury with the same facts. He listened intently and offered some desperately needed legal advice that afternoon, instructions on how to prepare for the trial. Then, the bluntness of his advice kept ringing in my ears.

"Your liberty's at stake here. Your life. Your children's lives, too. You have to go sit on your lawyer's doorstep and demand or plead that he devotes the next two weeks of his life to your case. If he doesn't, you're in big trouble. Even then, if he's not prepared, if you and your witnesses aren't prepared, you'll lose. Listen, prosecutors win weak cases all the time." He spoke softly but distinctly and with conviction. I felt so safe and wished he could be the one who would walk into court with us.

Gerald and I grew more frightened as the lawyer described how mortally serious our situation was. He said he wished he could give us the hope that we were looking for, the belief that the truth wins in cases like ours. But he said he couldn't. He explained how the jury only sees fragments of the story. "And sadly," he said, "unfortunately, we're not talking about justice here, we're talking about law." He gave us one final piece of advice. "You have to get your lawyer to subpoena those involved who can support the evidence that these are false charges. You just have to."

"And what if he won't do that? We have asked him over and over," Gerald explained.

"Then ask him why not. Get him to sign a piece of paper that says he won't subpoena who you ask and give it to the judge before the trial starts." He stood up and indicated that our time was up. He shook our hands. I didn't want to leave, but of course, we had no choice.

As we stepped out into the bitter cold again, we realized what we needed to do. Gerald promised to contact Ranski Monday morning, even if he had to "plant himself on his doorstep."

I drafted a letter like the one the lawyer advised us to write to the judge, just in case we needed it.

We drove toward my sister's to pick up Jonathan so he could spend the night, but stopped off to say hi to Lucy and Sanford. Like old times, Sanford treated us to some of his great cooking. He had just fried up a large skillet of fried chicken wings, so we all sat around savoring a late lunch and managed to get all caught up since the last time we saw them.

As soon as I saw Katie, I asked her if she was still using the bunk beds. She said yes, so I hurried upstairs and took some pictures with our camera which I had stuffed in my purse. I told Katie it was evidence that might help, along with the fact that in their depositions, the kids keep saying they never once saw any abuse.

After visiting for a short while, Jonathan jumped in the car with us and we drove toward home.

CHAPTER 18

G erald's lawyer consented to see us one week before the trial. The evening prior to our appointment with him, I scrutinized everything again and prepared an outline of various important points.

As we sat in the living room, Gerald shocked me with what I thought was an exceptional idea, if we had to use it as a last resort. "I'll tell you what I'm going to do, by God, if they convict me. I'm going to fast, that's it, stop eating until somebody takes a look at this," he said.

He sounded very serious about his plan.

"That's the best idea I've heard yet. I'll fast with you. That is a good idea, Ger. I mean if it should ever come to that. But, with these last depositions, and Cobers' report, honey, I'm telling you, it shouldn't ever come to that."

"Yeah, well all I know is I'm tired of it all, Karrol. I'm sick and tired of it taking up so much of our life, your time and mine. I mean it. One way or another, I want it all to end."

We sat across from each other once again, like so many times in the past, feeling frustrated and angry, wishing things could be different.

We awoke early and dressed quickly, since we were eager to meet with Ranski and finally discuss strategies.

I walked Angel, then coaxed her back inside. "C'mon girl, c'mon in." She continued to jump up and down so I gave her an ice cube to settle her down.

"Well, are you about ready?" Ger asked from the bathroom.

"Yeah, I'm ready whenever you are." I picked up a folder and large brown envelope full of papers to take to the lawyer. I also had a copy of the letter I had drawn up, written to the judge, about the issue of the subpoenas. But I kept it in my purse. We didn't want to utilize it, but we would if we felt it was necessary.

We listened to some soothing music on the way to Crestwood Edge, a Kenny G. cassette.

As we noticed a car in the ditch off to the right, as we drove along the expressway, it reminded Gerald of his shift at the hospital a few nights before. He spoke about several emergencies, an auto crash which killed a person, a little boy who had injured himself when the toilet seat came crashing down on him as he went to the bathroom, and an elderly woman who had suffered a heart attack, but looked like she would make it.

I told him the stories would make an interesting episode of "Rescue 911." "Except for the car wreck. I like the ones where they're okay in the end."

At 8:40 A.M., we parked the car at the lawyer's office. Gerald asked to see the latest material I had put together. "Let me look over that stuff one more time."

"Okay, here." I took the stapled six pages of paper out of the envelope and handed it to him. "Here's the chronological order of events and some information on the depositions."

As he read through the latest inconsistencies and falsehoods again, he remained silent except for a few sniffles.

By five till nine, we were eager and anticipating the consultation. We walked through the doorway, up the stairs and into his office and sat down. We perused several magazines and worked a crossword puzzle while waiting. Ranski had called to say he would be late. The longer we waited, the more anxiety crept up to remind us of the predicament which we faced.

Gerald grew more impatient with each passing minute. We sat and watched the doorway. Finally his lawyer walked in.

"Hi Gerald, sorry I'm late." He stepped through another doorway toward his office. He said, "C'mon in, Gerald. Can I talk to you alone first?"

Gerald looked at me, shrugged his shoulders, motioned to me that he would be okay, then went in.

I picked up another magazine, but set it back down. The rectangular clock to the left seemed to tick louder and louder. It wasn't long before I thought I could hear my own heart beat. The waiting room remained empty except for me. I kept crossing and uncrossing my legs.

Ten minutes passed. Suddenly, I began to shake. It dawned on me: they're in there talking deals again. Ger's so fed up and sick of it all, he's probably in there signing his life and dignity away, in a reckless, impatient moment, just to end it all right here and now.

I jumped up and tapped on the window. The friendly blond receptionist slid the glass open.

"Yes, uh, listen. Could you please do me a favor?"

She nodded. "Okay, right now, I need you to give my husband this message. Tell him if he signs anything without at least discussing it with me first, tell him I'll kill him."

"You'll kill him?" She smiled and obviously held back her instinct to laugh. She realized I was not serious, but that I certainly did want to relay the message.

"Yeah. Tell him that, okay?" I said with a laugh.

She returned right away still smiling. "You can go in now, Mrs. Karlin."

"Oh good, thanks." I sighed and felt immediate relief. Somehow I knew I had let my imagination get the best of me. At least I hoped so.

As I sat down, Ranski explained that it was his job to let Gerald know his options. He had spent more time trying to make Gerald understand that a guilty verdict and prison sentence still remained a strong possibility.

I tried to make myself comfortable by sitting next to Ger facing Ranski as we looked at him across his long, charcoal gray colored desk. There were manila folders stacked everywhere. It seemed every lawyer's office had them.

I looked at Gerald for some kind of explanation.

"I told him no, that we discussed it the other day and the subject of a plea bargain is closed. He was just letting me know that the option still existed. And we just started talking about the trial."

I looked back at Ranski as if to say, why are you mentioning deals again. He had another colorful tie on. That was another thing I had noticed about lawyers.

He defended his motives. "I was just letting him know that the option was still there. As his lawyer, I have to do that."

He went on to explain that the trial would start Monday, the 27th of February. "There will be no trial Tuesday because, I don't know, I think the judge has something else to do. Then we'll resume Wednesday and possibly, hopefully finish up on Thursday." He paused. "Oh, and the jury is chosen in the morning on the first day. That's how it's done," he explained.

"Yes, you said they did it that way, with the jury. And what about the kids, will they be in court?" Gerald asked.

"Yes. They'll be there."

"So they will have to say this stuff in front of Gerald then?" Ger had always worried about that. He felt the kids would get up on the stand and be compelled to finally spit out the truth and at that point they might be in danger. He worried that if the kids told the truth and things started looking bad for Flora, maybe she would hurt them, or they'd have to pay somehow for their honesty. We couldn't protect them, because nobody would listen to us.

But lately, after seeing the kids ignore us at the courthouse and with their latest depositions, even with Gerald's presence, I felt that the kids were too far gone and sadly, even in front of their dad, they probably weren't going to hesitate to say what they had so dutifully learned.

One question after another came out of Gerald's mouth. We went back and forth and I began to feel more confident and upbeat for a change. According to the conversation, Gerald's tone of voice and Ranski's concession to participate and work with us, it seemed as if we were finally joining forces. As our meeting progressed, we began to feel more hopeful that the momentum could shift in our direction, the direction of justice.

"I think you did a good job, by the way, with the kids, and their mom on the depositions. There's some powerful stuff there too, don't you think?" It was easy to be critical and irritated so often, I had to complement Ranski on the way he had handled the kids.

"Yes I do. Like we've said with the kids, certain things simply don't add up. I mean they are convincing sometimes, but I think we have some strong points for reasonable doubt. And with regard to Todd, you saw how, well, the way he kept getting so defensive, couldn't answer some questions and just kept wanting to end it. If we can get him like that again, it will probably help."

158

Ranski continued to mention another important point, Flora's hostility toward Gerald. "I mean we're just asking her about certain dates and things that happened, and she just keeps acting more hostile towards you. And with her inconsistencies and inability to remember things, she doesn't make a very credible witness."

I reminded Ranski of one of the most memorable inconsistencies, the fact that Flora tells two different versions of how she first learned of the abuse by Gerry. I said, "I would think if your child comes to you and lets you know he or she's been abused, you're going to remember exactly where and when you were at that moment in time. But you see, that's the thing, she bounces around from one therapist or doctor to the next and tells them different things. Can't you bring this out?" I asked.

He said he could try. Then Ranski explained how Dr. Cobers would serve a double purpose, as the psychologist who was first asked to evaluate the boys, and the one who supports Gerald's innocence and as an educator. "She's going to explain the syndromes and how some children believe the abuse to be real sometimes, when it never happened. Oh, and by the way, the prosecutor, she's calling and telling me she hasn't had a chance to depose Dr. Cobers. She set it up for one time and Dr. Cobers explained that she was busy and unavailable. So now she's saying well, she can't depose Cobers on Friday because she has a job interview. Well, I've got news for her, the judge isn't going to care about her job interview when she's had all this time to obtain the deposition." Ranski kept giving us more interesting information.

"Gee, now I wonder why she doesn't want to depose Dr. Cobers," Gerald said facetiously.

Then Gerald and Ranski took turns making one point after another. I listened and tried to absorb it all. We all agreed that there was a long road ahead of us with the boys. An acquittal would only be the beginning.

Ranski continued to hedge about the subpoenas, when we started in on that topic. He stated that CPS never shows up anyway. We understood that many of their witnesses would be our witnesses too, but according to the lawyer in Kellton, we stressed again, the importance of calling in certain people, to support Gerald's innocence.

We wanted to utilize the policeman who took the kids' statements, since he had said he had some doubts and we wanted to bring in some family and neighbors, all who would testify that the kids seemed happy with us.

Then Gerald remembered something else. "You know, Walter, I just realized something else the other day, another reason I want you to subpoena Ralston, you know, one of the boys' therapists from Dr. Tano's. Because while Flora was saying I did this, she was calling me up on the phone and asking me to take the kids to their appointments there at Tanos'. I sat in the office and..."

"Wait a minute," Ranski interrupted to clarify what Ger was implying. "Are you saying that she was calling you up and asking you to take the kids to their appointments and she had already alleged the abuse?" Finally it had dawned on him that Flora's behavior was inconsistent with a mother who feared abuse of her children and wanted to protect them.

"That's right," Gerald said. "That's what we've been trying to tell people all along. If she's telling people she stopped visitation when she first started in with this pack of nonsense, then they'd better think again, because we can certainly prove that is not true. One of the people on the grand jury even asked about that, if she had ever returned the kids after claiming abuse. Well, I'll say she did. You just look at that list, the chronological order of things and see how much we had the boys." Gerald took a deep breath. "So subpoena him, okay. You said you couldn't find his telephone number, but I found it. I've written it down there for you." Gerald made his last strong point of defense and requests.

"Following what felt like a productive, mostly upbeat meeting, Gerald and Ranski shook hands before we left. He asked Ranski to refrain from mentioning any more plea bargains. He said we'd see him at the trial, and be ready to win.

As we walked out of the office, I smiled again at the receptionist.

While walking to the car, I said, "Hey Ger, don't forget, we're going to church Sunday morning. You don't work, do you?" I waited for his response.

"Sorry, hon, but I'm scheduled. How about the Sunday after that?" He unlocked my door and opened it. I climbed in and unlocked his side.

"Oh darn it. Oh well, next Sunday then. Sadie says there's going to be some really great music that day, so that will be even better I guess. But I wanted to go before Monday, before the trial, you know." I buckled in and got comfortable.

"You don't have to go to church you know. God knows, honey. He knows." He sounded confident that God would be there for him in his greatest hour of need. "That was a quality meeting with him, huh?"

"Yeah, it was. We talked about an awful lot of stuff, didn't we?"

"We sure did. I'm still concerned somewhat about those subpoenas, but I do feel a lot better, how about you? Glad I didn't sign anything?" He teased, knowing very well I did not want to hear any mention of any types of deals. As far as I was concerned, it would be a contract with the devil, a selling of his soul.

"I don't even want to joke about it, honey," I said seriously.

We managed to remain in good spirits for the long drive home and the rest of the evening.

CHAPTER 19

Gerald and I tried to remain positive and hopeful, but we grew more restless as the week dragged on. On Wednesday evening, one comment led to another and before we knew it the discussion centered around the boys again and our self doubts about being able to turn everything around.

"This waiting around and never getting anywhere is killing me. I just want to walk in there and get it over with." Gerald really let it out that night. All of his frustrations seemed to surface after trying to suppress everything for so long. "I don't know, I'm just so afraid that the boys are going to be so messed up after this. I'm beginning to feel the madness, the revolting sick reality of what's going on here, and I just can't take it much longer." He hung his head down and put his hand over his forehead. I imagined how devastating it all was to him, but only he knew how deeply his spirit had been damaged and if a reservoir of strength and faith of some sort remained that could help see him through the nightmare.

On Thursday night, somehow he managed to follow through with teaching a CPR class at the hospital. I drove over to pick him up. While I waited in the car, I thought about what a great instructor people would lose if he ended up in prison. But then I realized, he'd probably find some way to instruct even the inmates on the virtues and skills of cardiopulmonary resuscitation and first aid.

The night remained calm and uneventful. However, it marked the deceptive calm before the roughest storm yet. Gerald still looked dead tired. He took a couple of Tylenol for his headache and fell asleep.

As I tossed and turned, intuition, that remarkable inner most gut feeling hinted that something was about to go wrong. I knew that things would not go forth smoothly or as planned.

On Friday evening, I received the dreaded phone call, the phone call that never should have happened, not from Gerald's lawyer. We had just started to believe in him.

As I held the receiver to my ear, I heard him talking. My breathing became more shallow. My heart seemed to skip beats. The kitchen lighting grew dimmer as darkness fell and the conversation so coldly reminded me that the war between good and evil, between right and wrong, is so ghastly complicated and relentless.

I fully understood the possible consequences of continuing our fight for the truth. Gerald, an innocent man, my loving husband, could be sent to prison. Another option was surrender. But I realized a long time ago that the haunting dilemma which we had unfairly faced for years was an all or nothing situation.

But now they were pressuring Ger again, offering him another deal.

"Look, Mrs. Karlin," Ranski professed. "He can take this, two counts of battery, it's a Class A Misdemeanor, the sexual aspect has been excluded, then he won't go to jail and he can go back into family court and fight it."

Thoroughly disgusted, disappointed, and not believing a word of it, I refuted every point Ranski brought up as he argued for my husband to give in and plea bargain his life away.

Finally I said, "Look, Gerald won't be home until after midnight, so you'll have to call him tomorrow or leave a number where he can call you." The conversation literally made me sick to my stomach. I grabbed my abdomen and knew I would have to take some Pepto-Bismol.

"Okay. I'll tell you what. I'll call him about 10 A.M., all right?"

"Yeah fine. Good-bye." I felt like Ger and I needed to buckle in for another roller coaster ride.

I hurried to the bathroom, took two large swigs of Pepto, curled up on the couch under an afghan and began to shiver. It was obvious. Ger and I had nobody to help us. We were all alone again. Gerald deserved better, not this betrayal at the last minute. An ultimate fear consumed me. Would Gerald weaken and accept their lousy deal?

An hour later, I managed to turn a light switch on and move to the phone at the kitchen table. I dialed a number out of the yellow pages, like so often before. Sometimes the lawyer would talk to me, sometimes they wouldn't. I knew I'd have to get lucky to reach anyone after six. All the second opinion lawyer had to do to make up my mind was to reinforce everything I already believed to be true. His words of wisdom were just what I needed at such a critical point in time. And I also needed someone to say, 'Hang in there. Don't give up the fight.' After all, if everyone keeps telling you to just give it up, then what's the point?

I paced, thought, agonized as my stomach continued to churn. It still hurt. I needed some fresh air, so I walked Angel. That's when the notion hit me, the parallel between legal and sexual abuse. Gerald was being pressured to submit. It was as if he had no rights, no power, except to say no. He could still say no. But would he?

Later in the evening, as I watched a documentary on Rosa Parks, I thought of the prosecutor and Ranski again, this time as the unfair, righteous oppressors. They would do anything to try and force Gerald to 'give up his seat,' to give up his worth as a human being and his will to fight for what is right. If they succeeded, I vowed right then and there, to sit down in the seat instead. I decided that life is too precious to be crushed by injustice. I didn't have as much to lose. I would not go to jail. I wondered where the competent prosecutors and lawyers were.

Ger returned home from work about 1 A.M. He was obviously ready to sleep, nothing more. I had no intention of ruining his chance for some rest. Instead, I woke him up earlier than planned, to inform him of the phone call last night and the fact that Ranski would be calling about ten for his decision. Only Gerald could make a choice so intimately connected with his conscience and future. I knew that.

"However," I explained, "I see this case like a disease, and you deserve a second opinion. So I want you to do me a favor, listen to what your lawyer has to say, then read what the second lawyer said when I called him last night. Then I'm going to take Angel, leave for a while and you can take some time to make up your mind. And whatever you decide, "I'll understand, and I'll always love you Ger, no matter what."

He listened. We kissed. I knew it would be rough for him, and I knew how tired he was, how he just wanted it to end. I felt really scared. I drove down the rode toward the veterinarians with Angel in the back seat, listening to my Tracy Chapman tape.

Upon returning, as I stepped up to open the door, I heard Gerald talking on the phone. I knew it was his lawyer, and it didn't sound good. I opened the door, let Angel inside, walked back out and shuffled aimlessly down the street.

It was evident that he was about to surrender. He had fought long and hard, so I couldn't blame him. Certainly, I would always love him, but a sense of defeat overwhelmed me.

About ten minutes later, I walked in and blurted out, "So what's it gonna be, are we going to trial on Monday or not?" I tried to prepare for the awful words of surrender that would come next.

"No. I just can't fight any more. I want it to be over with, Karrol. Please understand. They've dropped the sexual abuse and I can go back to family court and fight it." He looked at me for understanding.

At first I was stunned, then angry and I knew there was no way I could agree with his decision. He had every right to make up his own mind, but I knew giving up was not something that I could do.

I couldn't help sounding bitter and disappointed." You think you can go back into family court. You think you'll be a paramedic student. You think you'll be teaching still and be able to get a job and get your kids back, your life back someday. But what did that other lawyer tell us? He said you sign and it's all over, didn't he?"

"Well, I just don't want to go to prison. You said you'd understand." Now he sounded disappointed and wanted to know where my promises had gone.

"I do understand. That doesn't mean I have to agree." I paced back and forth as we both tried to explain ourselves.

Gerald told me that he didn't have any confidence in Ranski, and I couldn't blame him. He said if Ranski acted like he would try and get the facts out in the open and try his best to defend

166

him, then he might feel like he had a chance. But he had no faith that he would even try, not after the last phone call.

He looked at me in bewilderment. "And he told me about a case where a guy was charged with rape and there was a lot of reasonable doubt that he did it. They proved it. But he's still rotting in prison somewhere, right now. That's what really did it, when he told me about that case."

I explained again that it was his decision. Only he could make it, since he was the one facing prison. "But you see," I said, "I'm not facing prison, and I refuse to give into this nonsense. So from this moment on I have to do what I feel is best. I intend to fast in protest of you signing any deals, and I'll fast as long as it takes for somebody to review this case impartially, until somebody out there listens to the truth, because I know that you never abused Todd and Gerry. I was there, remember?"

He looked utterly puzzled and angered by what I was telling him. "Oh, goddamn it, Karrol, please don't do this. Please don't put this kind of pressure on me. God, I can't, I just can't go through this any more." He began to plead with me, almost cry.

"I'm sorry Ger, really. But what kind of life do you think you, us, the kids are gonna have after you sign this? I think surrendering to the madness, as you called it, will eventually destroy us." Sadly, I had no assurances that continuing to fight would eventually empower us to fare much better.

"I'm telling you I can't take any more of this. I have no confidence in my lawyer, what the hell am I supposed to do? You see how he fights us on every fact or idea we give him, all the evidence. He acted like he was ready to go to bat for me on Monday; now this. He says I've got a good chance of ending up in jail because the kids are so convincing." As he spoke, I could see he was in turmoil. They had backed him into a corner. I had reached my limitations many times, now he was reaching his. Innocent victims can only take so much, fight so long, I realized that.

I proceeded to tell him how dearly I loved him, but I, too, had made my decision and I had no intentions of backing down.

I laid down the rules of my plan. In protest of Gerald being pressured to sign and agreeing to sign a plea agreement, I would fast. The fast would end only when Gerald changed his mind or when an impartial investigation was initiated.

"Because I am certain an impartial investigation will exonerate you and prove all of these charges were malicious and false. Maybe that lawyer was wrong, the one who said if you sign, it's all over. Maybe if I'm dying in a hospital somewhere, they'll finally do the right thing and finally listen to your side of the story, look at the facts. Maybe not. Maybe some of the professionals involved in this, our neighbors, friends, family, people who know the abuse did not happen, maybe they will all come forward finally and force someone to help the kids and us." I rambled on.

"Why are you doing this, Karrol? Why are you doing this to me?" he asked.

"At this point, it's not about you. It's about me. I admit it's selfish, but it's also about us. Because, maybe you can go on about your daily business without believing in anything. Maybe you can do that. I can't. You want to know what it's about? When I see our country flag blowing in the wind, I want to feel a sense of pride and trust. Because I'm no good to anybody if I can't believe in the goodness of the world." I told him again how I loved him with all my heart. Usually he expressed the same sentiment in return, but he remained silent.

With the silence, I began my protest. The 2% milk, some left over chicken and noodles, the Eckrich sausage, the eggs, and Oscar Mayer bologna, even the box of butterscotch pudding all remained untouched from 11:20 A.M. Saturday until Sunday evening at seven o'clock. I didn't even chew a piece of gum. Water became my only intake, my only source of replenishment.

Poor Gerald teeter tottered back and forth. Now he felt pressured not to submit.

"And what about prison," he raised his eyebrows and looked deadly serious as he stood in the hallway, "what about what I'll have to go through in there?"

"I don't want you to go to prison either. I don't. I only know that if we fight, we have a chance. It may not end here, before you get unjustly shuffled off to prison. But if we don't give up, I believe that in time, there will be some positive resolutions. If we take the dead end shortcut and it's all over with, then they win. The kids will be goners and I know it will destroy us." I gave it my best shot and tried to make him see some sense in continuing our fight for the truth.

"Well," I felt him coming back to me, "you realize if I'm found guilty, they're going to take me away right there on the spot." He began to prep me for the worst case scenario.

"God, I don't want to ever lose you, sweetheart, not for a second. You know that, right?"

"Yeah." We walked closer toward each other and embraced. "Hey, all I have to do, when I go in is tell 'em I feel like committing suicide and they'll isolate me, so I won't have to be subjected to any shit. And if we have to, we'll just fast until somebody listens."

My Rosa Parks was back. The phone rang at 7 P.M. Gerald gave Ranski the news, "Yeah, well, I've changed my mind. There isn't going to be any deal. When the prosecutor wants to drop these charges or I'm found not guilty, after people listen to the facts, the truth, that's the deal I'll take," Gerald stated proudly with conviction. He paused, then sighed. "Look," he spoke into the receiver, "I've heard your arguments on the matter. I want my day in court. So I'll see you at 8:30 in the morning then at my trial. Okay? Bye." He hung up.

I was never so anxious and relieved in my entire life.

"Well, I'll tell you, he's not very happy right now," Gerald said seriously as he opened the refrigerator door.

I laughed a little, "No I guess he's not, now he's got to work on his opening all night. They aren't ready, him or the prosecutor, because they never intended this to go to trial. Never."

"Hey, do me a favor. Eat, will you?" He pointed at the food sitting on the shelves.

"Oh boy, that's right. I can eat again." I grabbed the bologna and small plastic container of mustard. "God, I love you," I said, then kissed him on the cheek.

"I love you too, Karrol. God how I'd be feeling right now if I had signed that. Thanks." He sighed. "Eat. Eat!"

We sat down at the kitchen table while I ate my sandwich. We held hands and smiled at each other.

A little later, I went to the bedroom and looked in the closet to pick out something to wear to court. Gerald had me press his dark blue pants and light blue shirt.

As I ironed, I thought, what a roller coaster ride.

When I called Katie, she said she could get a babysitter and meet us at the courthouse, but I explained how the first part of the morning would probably be spent picking a jury. So I told her to just sit tight, and I would call her if I needed her to come for the first day.

In fact, I called everybody and told them to plan on coming the second day of the trial instead, which would be Wednesday.

CHAPTER 20

Once again reunited and firmly resolved to do the right thing, Gerald and I took it one step at a time as we entered the court house on Monday morning, February 27th, 1995, to face our destiny.

I wore my black skirt and sweater. Mourning colors seemed appropriate for the serious occasion. Gerald dressed in dark blue pants, a light blue shirt, suit coat and a colorful tie. His wavy brown hair was neatly combed. He looked very professional, as if he belonged at a business meeting rather than in court, sitting on a hot seat.

We stood outside the court room until 8:25 A.M., then we went in and sat down. Judge Westley entered soon after, and as commanded to, we all rose. Gerald and I noticed the prisoners dressed in blue off to the right, and listened as the proceedings began. Ranski was no where in sight, which made us nervous.

Our adversary, the deputy prosecutor, addressed the court on behalf of the State, while defense lawyers argued for their clients. Occasionally, she looked back and we made eye contact. There was no doubt in my mind that she was disappointed that Gerald had decided to continue his fight. I firmly believed that both the prosecutor and Ranski were not ready to proceed with the trial.

The judge's words echoed in my ears, "The burden of proof lies with the State. That never changes."

Suddenly Ranski snuck up behind us. "Hi, Gerald, can I talk to you for a second?" he whispered. I thought to myself, this isn't good. I heard the essence of the conversation before the familiar bailiff came over and instructed Gerald and his lawyer to utilize the small enclosed quarters in the back of the courtroom if they wanted to continue to talk.

Gerald came back and motioned for me to step outside. As quietly as I could, I inched my way toward the back of the room, then pushed through the door.

"Yeah, he says that after he spoke with me last night, the prosecutor received a call from Dr. Edison, the one they're flying in to testify. Well, his father died and he won't be able to come Wednesday. So they are going to ask for another continuance." Gerald explained the situation as we stood in the corridor.

"Well, ask them if the doctor can come on Thursday or Friday then. This isn't fair, Walter. You have to tell the judge how long Ger's waited for his day in court."

I looked at Gerald. It was obvious that neither one of us felt as if we could tolerate yet another delay.

Mr. Ranski explained, "But it's not up to me. I can tell them we are not in agreement with the continuance, but it's not up to me. The judge probably isn't going to allow a trial to start if one of the main witnesses can't be here."

With the bad news, we hurried in to sit back down. Following the initial shock concerning another delay, both Gerald and I admitted that we too wanted Dr. Edison to appear. After all, we believed he was the medical doctor who could help prove our case, not the prosecutor's.

I literally sat on the edge of my seat and waited as Gerald stood beside Ranski before Judge Westley.

The deputy prosecutor spoke confidently, then stamped a piece of paper and walked toward the judge after explaining that Dr. Edison was in the midst of making funeral arrangements since his father had passed away. "So the State is asking for a continuance, Sir, in the case of the State vs. Gerald Karlin." She slowly walked back, stood behind her chair and awaited an approval.

Judge Westley leaned back and looked over the paper while remaining silent. Finally he said, "And Mr.Ranski. Now, what do you have to say with regard to a continuance?"

Given his opportunity to speak up, barely audibly, Ranski replied, "Yes, well, your honor, we have no objections to the continuance." Gerald and I had decided that we needed Dr. Edison too, but, we were hoping that at least the judge would be reminded of the numerous continuances Gerald had already endured.

My husband stood stoically awaiting the judge's next move. Still leaning forward on my seat, I placed my left hand over my forehead and shook my head several times back and forth. My arms rested on the back of the chair in front of me. Get a hold of yourself Karrol, I thought. We need Dr. Edison too. Ranski's not really prepared, maybe this is for the best. A couple of weeks extension won't be the end of the world. I looked up and Judge Westley kept turning one page after another in his calendar book.

"Well," he said to the prosecutor, "You have to understand my problem here." Then I failed to hear what he said next. I only noticed that he continued to turn pages. During all of the long minutes of waiting and disappointment, I wondered, why doesn't Ranski speak up and tell them how long we have waited. He could remind him that at some point in time the court needs to recognize the forgotten concept of innocent until proven guilty. Gerald's stance is that these charges are false and that his kids need the proper help now.

Then the judge spoke up. "Well, May 30th, that's the best I can do."

When I realized that he had completely passed up all of March and April, and almost the whole month of May, I raised my hand spontaneously like a third grader. "Your honor, could I say something?"

But it was no use. Judge Westley soon realized, thanks to the prosecutor's help, that I was the 'wife of the accused.' He directed his comment to Mr. Ranski and told him to interview me, since I had something to say. Gerald and Mr. Ranski glanced at me and wanted to say sit down and shut up. That's what I did, feeling totally defeated once more.

With the judge's decision, our chance to resolve our crisis disappeared again. I sat there in a daze for a few moments, until I heard Gerald say, "C'mon Karrol, let's go."

Again we stood in the corridor with Ranski. "I just wanted the judge to know how long we have waited. Why didn't you say anything?" I asked angrily.

"Well, the judge knows how long. He knows all that."

"Well I think the court needs to be reminded. You could still say it on Gerald's behalf."

"Look," Ranski said," there's one thing we don't want to do, that's get this judge irritated at us, okay?"

"Yes, I know. I know. But my God, three months?" I whined.

Gerald blurted out, "Really. This is getting pretty ridiculous."

"Ger, how can we live with this for three more months? I can't live with it another day!"

"I don't know, honey. I just don't know anymore."

As Gerald's words faded, we all turned toward the stairs to see what the commotion was. A crowd of potential jurors had evidently showed up as ordered. For the next few minutes we sat on a nearby bench and discussed several specific things and made some more of our same requests. We did our best to quickly review some of the evidence with Ranski, to make certain he knew what we thought was important to support Gerald's innocence. Then I pulled out a photo of the bunk bed. My sister had dismantled them to make two single beds, but we explained that we had always used them as bunk beds. I told Mr. Ranski that I would be picking up a receipt for the date that we bought the beds in a few days, and I would mail him a copy. It would show that we never had the beds in the room at the time when Todd said the abuse took place.

Finally, Gerald asked fairly graciously about the subpoenas again. "Hey, okay, now we've got this extra time, what do you say, you'll go ahead and subpoena the people we need, right? Can you do that?"

"I can do that," he finally conceded, which left me to worry and wonder if anyone had been subpoenaed already or not.

"Good. Thank you," Ger and I said in unison.

Then Gerald ended our discussion with Ranski by saying, "If they get in court and try to prove this, they're going to look stupid. That's all there is to it. And they're going to lose. We are going to win this thing. So when they drop these false charges or when I'm found guilty, tell them, that's when it will be over. And I don't want to hear anymore, please, no more about any deals. Okay?"

I walked away feeling proud of Gerald for speaking up and for gracefully accepting another setback, better than I could.

Later in the day, as we tried to relax at home again, we began to feel more optimistic about the turn of events. Especially, Ger realized that he had scored a victory simply by deciding to hang on and fight. He appeared more committed than ever to pursue justice.

After calling everyone we felt we needed to, we both began to adjust to the idea of living in limbo a while longer. Gerald studied the various kind of anatomical tissues and felt the need to share the 'interesting' knowledge he was absorbing. I found it amazing that he could actually concentrate on his studies.

In response, I asked him how he could possibly remember so much information and ramble it off like it was a second language. I was so happy for him. On Thursday evening he would be taking a test instead of possibly sitting in a jail cell somewhere feeling like the world and God had betrayed him.

The next morning, my co-workers welcomed me back. It was a good feeling to see all of their smiling faces. They deserved some type of explanation regarding my time off, so I told them.

"I'm back. Plans have changed once again. I'll be here the rest of the week after all. It involves a long drawn out visitation fight for our kids, Ger's sons. That's what it is, more or less." I took a deep breath and exhaled. "You have no idea, no idea what we have been through."

They were sympathetic. Of course, they had no way to know how complicated the whole mess had become.

A little later, I peeked around the doorway into my boss' office. "You know, it's more complicated than just a visitation issue. I'll tell you about it someday, when the time is right."

"Hmm. Maybe I don't want to know," she replied, which indicated to me that she had probably guessed what might be involved.

"No, you probably don't." I went back to my office, shut the door and sat in my chair and felt like I was still spinning from the roller coaster ride which we experienced. It was difficult to focus, but I got to work with some things that had to be done. The kind, elderly voices I heard over the telephone helped to redirect my thoughts, temporarily, anyway. For the last half hour at work, though, I called several toll free numbers which dealt with child abuse and protection. For some strange reason, I was trying to get help again, but I knew better. Nobody would step in at this point, not until Gerald was found not guilty.

Just before I left, Sadie handed me a fax which informed me of an upcoming seminar. Shortly after four o'clock I was back home. Ger continued to cram for his Anatomy and Physiology test while I stared at the television and kept reflecting. One thing we had mentioned to Ranski, was the idea of reverting back to a bench trial, leaving the verdict up to one intelligent judge who would hopefully review the facts of the case. I wondered how long it would take Ranski to get back to us. He said he would speak to a few fellow attorneys about it.

We weren't so sure the jury would see all of the evidence. I had read a few articles on juries, which did not ease my anxiety, and Ger had confided in a couple of nursing friends. They all said the same thing: "If the kids get up there and cry or tell what they believe happened convincingly, they're going to win the jury's sympathy."

So I asked Gerald, "What if the kids don't ever cry? What about the fact that they ramble this stuff off lately like they're talking about something so remote? Something, by the way, that they say happened and yet so many of their answers are inconsistent with other things they've said or just don't make sense."

I laid on the couch, mulling over the facts. I was the one who got up and down at night, Ger sleeps like a baby. I was the one who got the kids cereal in the mornings and turned on the cartoons for them, and then later in the morning watched them trot off happily and healthily with their dad to the Y.M.C.A.

So often I'd profess to Gerald, "If reasonable doubt doesn't exist in your case, especially with Dr. Cobers' report, then God help us all."

But I also remembered Gerald's haunting words about utilizing our key witness. Ranski had explained to him that Cobers could talk about some of the syndromes and lead right up to the point of saying the kids may have them, but she apparently could not actually come right out and say, "yes, that is what is happening right now, with these boys, in this particular case."

Of course I made it a point to remind Gerald and Ranski that the whole point of the psychologist's intervention was to evaluate, draw conclusions and make recommendations, and Dr. Cobers had done just that. It wasn't fair that all of a sudden, everyone wanted to ignore the role which she had played.

That was the point in time when I began to distrust the idea of a jury. Ranski couldn't promise that the jury would see or read Dr. Cobers' report. All the evidence, he said, would be there for them to look over, but he couldn't promise that they would read it. It didn't help either when I read one article which stated that jurors only hear fifteen percent of the trial.

When I heard the whistling from "The Andy Griffith Show," I got up to start supper. Angel began to wake up so Gerald moved his legs aside so she could get out from underneath his feet.

"Hey, Angel girl, you have to go outside, hmm?" He walked to the front door and let her out.

"Love you." I grabbed his hand as he passed by.

"Love you too, sugar. It's good to be home. Shoot, now I have to take my test. I thought I'd be in jail and wouldn't have to worry about it." He laughed.

After supper, I laid on the couch and watched a special about Shirley Temple, while he continued to study.

The phone rang. "Hi, Rennie. I tried to reach you last night. It's been continued again because one of the doctor's, his father passed away." I sat at the kitchen table annoyed at the static in the telephone. "This dumb phone. We have to get a new one. I know it's the phone."

"Continued again? Well I was thinking about you guys all day long. When's it gonna be then?" he asked.

"Well, are you ready for this? Not until May 30th."

He sounded genuinely sorry, but explained that he could not make the trial at that time, because someone from work would be on vacation. I told him we understood, that we knew they couldn't all be expected to schedule their lives around our court dates.

"But we wanted you to be around as a witness to tell how the kids were fine on Father's Day, you know, right before they went into the hospital."

"Well, we'll see. Maybe I can take a half day off or something. But really, Karrol, that's sure the week he'll be gone. But I'll try."

We both laughed when I told him it could be the next century, rather than May, before we had to show up again. We talked a little more and hung up.

The next day at work, I couldn't resist. I wrote a letter to the woman from Cardinal City who had spoken at the forum. I also sent a copy to the governor. It made me feel better.

For the next few days and throughout the weekend, the possibilities really sunk in. If the trial had taken place, maybe we would be feeling free again and we would be sitting in some lawyer's office asking for Ger's right to walk back into family court. Or Gerald and I could have been tragically torn apart from each other while he was dragged off to the tormenting reality of a prison cell. And Angel and I would be looking around every corner at home wondering why Gerald's presence had suddenly disappeared.

I managed to get back into the swing of things again at work.

Then amazingly, one morning as I traveled toward a clinic to attend a seminar, I happened to come across a show on the radio called, Focus on the Family. Within minutes, I had to pull into a bank parking lot because I was in tears.

The program panel members spoke so profoundly about the very ordeal we had been facing for so long, what happens when people are falsely accused. I didn't want to cry too much and end up with red and puffy eyes, but I was so emotionally affected by what was being said.

One professional stressed the point that sexual abuse is very real sometimes and we should never undermine that. Nobody disagreed. But the emphasis of the program centered around false claims and the way some victims are convinced the abuse was real, when it never really happened. There is such a thing as false memory and coercive therapies. Sometimes, it was explained, well-intended therapists prod and plant suggestions, beliefs of abuse. I thought about how the boys had denied it, but nobody would listen and sadly, over a period of time, how they finally gave in.

One victim of coercive therapy even won a large lawsuit on that issue against a therapist. The victim later became what's called a 'retractor,' someone who retracts the accusation because the person finally realizes the accusations were not true. But sadly, sometimes that doesn't happen because the accuser is convinced that the abuse was real.

They also pointed out that sometimes the false memories develop separate from therapy sessions, in dreams or thoughts. Then I heard a Dr. Paul Simpson speak, and what he explained dealt with the saddest part about our case. He had counseled someone for three years and never listened to the other person's side of the story, the person accused. He stated, "You tend to get a very skewed perspective this way."

"Skewed," I thought, that's definitely the problem. If those prosecuting cases which involve families involved in divorces would stop for just one second to think about the aspect of motivation from the accuser, some tragic stories might be prevented. After all, don't children of divorced parents have enough to deal with already?

As I sat listening intently to every word, I began to feel a sense of hope. I had often wondered, how would Gerald and the kids ever regain a sense of trust and the love that they once shared. So often, Ger would say he realized that there was nothing to blame Todd or Gerry for, "They're just innocent victims who can't really grasp what's going on." But he was skeptical about the possibility of repairing all the damage that had been done to the boys, as well as his relationship with his sons.

The radio program mentioned Project Middle Ground, located in Tucson, Arizona. It sounded like the kind of help we all needed. As I noticed the time and looked in the mirror to check my eyes, I said a little thank you to God for making sure that I had tuned into the right station. I experienced a renewed sense of hope, too, since it seemed like the right kind of help was out there waiting for us.

Luckily, I was only a few minutes late. When I walked in, I saw all of my fellow community service workers. The topic was dementia. The speaker was very animated and interesting, so I managed to focus for the most part. But I couldn't help to drift off on occasion and think about how remarkable the radio program was that I had just heard.

Then a disturbing memory came to mind, a T.V. special about foster kids. I wondered how the abuse issue had ever gotten so complicated. The first I had heard about false allegations was from the foster-adoptive parent who had founded VOCAL. He said that some kids in foster care use the system to their advantage. If they don't like it somewhere, all they have to do is make up something. But the show I saw dealt with kids who had been in the system for years and they claimed that they would tell and tell about actual abuse, over and over, and nobody ever listened or did a thing about it.

So I wondered about foster care situations and cases like ours, how deciphering the truth had turned into a much more difficult and crucial task.

CHAPTER 21

G ray skies and rain monopolized the month of April, and we had more bad luck with the car, brake troubles. Gerald picked up more hours at both jobs, but financial stress continued to haunt us. We still had a long way to go before family and friends would be paid back. But, we thought, if we could just hang in there, merely survive economically, a little while longer, the gas and electric bills would be caught up and much lower with warmer weather, and soon, our car would be paid off.

We spent our time day after day, month after month, prior to the trial, working and carrying out the mundane tasks in order to keep a household running fairly smoothly. Occasionally, we even managed to enjoy a country drive or take in a bargain-priced movie.

One Friday evening, we jointly tackled the job of laundry. "Here hon," I said, "give her this, maybe she'll chew on it for awhile." I tossed Gerald one of Angel's chicken basted bones.

"Oh, okay," he said as he caught the bone." All she wants to do is play anymore. Right girl, here ya go." Angel snatched it from his hands, plopped down in the middle of the living room floor and began to chew.

"Did you get the basket from underneath the sink in the bathroom?" I asked.

"No, I didn't, and I forgot the hangers. Could you grab some? I'm going to check the trunk to see if we have any soap left."

This should be fun, I thought to myself. He's got a system and I've got my own way of doing laundry. Sure enough, not long after we were at the laundromat, we began to delve into each other's systems.

"You can't put the socks in with the towels. I've got socks and underwear over here in this one. Let's keep 'em all together. Okay?" I pulled out the dirty socks.

As the clothes washed, Gerald played video games, while I sat and read a magazine. We managed to work together for the rest of the job, and finally arrived home to complete the chore. We tried our best to live each day, not just sit around and worry about the trial or fear the worst. Gerald's mind got pre-occupied with his paramedic studies. However, it concerned us that his lawyer seemed determined not to communicate with us. He did not return our phone calls. He did not send us certain information he had promised. Maybe he was doing something in preparation for Gerald's trial, but if so, we were not aware of anything.

One day, due to the frustration, Gerald called the Public Defender's office. They told him if he didn't like his lawyer, "then go hire another one." They also indicated that the judge did not like to receive letters about lawyers. Gerald explained that he did not want to complain or cause friction between himself and the person he had to depend on. But, we knew that if Mr. Ranski refused to subpoena people on Gerald's behalf, then at the next pre-trial, he would have no choice. It would then be necessary to inform the judge of the situation.

In the interim before the trial, I read parts of a book on the criminal justice system. It helped to put certain things in perspective. Mostly, it forced me to see both pros and cons, both sides to so many different issues dealing with criminals and victims, as well as the system itself.

I read more about the American jury system. I concluded that juries are only as reliable as the people who serve on them. And serving on a jury is probably like other jobs, in one respect. Some people take the job seriously and do their best, while others only work hard enough to pass the time and get by. I wondered, would Gerald be lucky or unlucky, with his jury selection?

Night after night, I prayed and asked God to see us through. Each passing day Gerald and I spent together became more precious, because as the awful threat of losing him grew nearer, it made me realize the urgency of savoring every moment, just in case.

When it started getting closer to the time for the next pre-trial, scheduled for May 12, I asked Gerald to call up Ranski and tell him to make sure he brings our photo album of the kids to the pre-trial. It would be no problem for us to have them on hand each day of the trial, in case they were needed.

We didn't know what to expect. Mr. Ranski had not responded to our phone calls or letters, nor had he sent any of the material we had requested, especially the feedback regarding the possibility of a bench trial. But we assumed it was too late for that idea.

After a couple of kisses on Gerald's cheek, I left for work. Around one o'clock, I returned for lunch. I heard Ger's voice as I walked up the steps. It was clear that he was talking with his lawyer.

As I walked in, Gerald stared at me, while continuing to hold the phone to his ear. His eyes were red and there was an expression on his face of joy and relief. He quickly said, "Okay then, thanks a lot. Goodbye."

Suddenly, I knew. "What? Tell me it's over, c'mon please, tell me it's all over with," I pleaded.

"It's over, sugar. It's over. My case has been dismissed." We threw our arms around each other and cried together, our long awaited tears of relief.

"For real? That's it, you're sure?"

"That's what Ranski just told me. I still have to go to court tomorrow, but it's been dismissed."

"Oh God, I can't believe it. I can't believe it. We can really go on with our lives now? Thank you God, thank you." We continued to embrace.

I felt like a team of doctors had just told Gerald and I that we were both cured of cancer. It was as if, in one transitional moment in time, my husband and I were once again welcomed by a world that for so long had seemed destined to abandon and punish us because of a lie.

"I don't know, Karrol, it's strange. It's like someone actually walked over and lifted some type of heavy weight off of me. You know when you squeeze your hand real hard, then finally open it and all the blood comes rushing back in. That's how it feels, too." He laid on the couch and looked so happy, so utterly relieved. I sat in the chair across from him while we talked and laughed and planned. It was wonderful. We were so thrilled and grateful, because somehow we had been given our lives, our chance for a future, back. Eventually I returned to work and breezed through the afternoon. Wild horses could not have kept me away from that courtroom on Friday morning. Even though we had won, I had the anxiety jitters all morning. "Let's leave early. What if we have a flat tire? What if Ranski is late again?" I paced back and forth after dressing an hour early.

"Settle down," Gerald said, "we'll get there. We'll get there. Calm down, Karrol." He looked so colorful and neat in his green-striped shirt.

"All right, but let's go." I grabbed my purse off of the kitchen table. Ger took a few more sips of coffee and obliged my request to hurry things along.

As we sat in the parking lot of the courthouse complex, we watched the employees flock in and completed the daily crossword puzzle. Everything seemed less ominous that day, even as we walked through the security detector. The guard joked with us about the thought of having to search through the entire contents of my purse. Since it did not set off any alarms, he took one glance and let me pass.

We were early. Gerald walked back downstairs to smoke another cigarette, while I decided to take a good seat.

I kept my eyes open for the new deputy prosecuting attorney who had evidently played a role in saving my husband's life. Apparently the other one had run off to another job and dumped Gerald's case right into the new prosecutor's lap. Some follow through, I thought. It sure makes a person wonder. But then, it was good for us, whatever the reasons for her last minute jumping of the ship.

The judge walked in. We all stood up, then sat back down. Our nightmare seemed much closer to ending, but as feared, Ranski was no where to be found. One by one, lawyer and client stood before Judge Westley, as we had to sit and wait.

The new prosecutor appeared very young. He had short, neatly cut brown hair and wore a gray suit and reddish tie. He sipped coffee, nibbled on his pen and occasionally walked confidently up to hand the judge certain papers.

184

I nudged Gerald and whispered, "If he doesn't show up, just tell the judge your lawyer's not here, you're representing yourself now and you want to proceed. Okay?"

"Okay, no problem," he whispered back.

It was moments later we heard, "Gerald Karlin." Gerald walked confidently toward the area he was directed to and took his place. "Mr. Karlin, the State has dismissed your case." As the Judge spoke those wonderful words, the prosecuting attorney took a couple of steps toward Gerald and handed him a piece of paper. Gerald looked at the paper for a minute or so, then said, "Is that it then?" The prosecutor nodded and we were free to go. Finally.

I stood up and whispered an ecstatic, "Yes!" I smiled directly at Judge Westley who still looked somewhat perplexed by the whole ordeal.

We stepped out into the corridor. We didn't cry and hugged only for a moment. I think we were too stunned and wondering if it all was actually happening.

"I hope this isn't a dream and we're about to wake up any minute," I said to Gerald who kept his head down and continued to study the paper he had received. Suddenly he said, "Hey, there's no signature on this. The judge hasn't signed it." He turned back toward the courtroom.

"Oh no. Hurry, go check it out," I prodded." We ran into that problem before, remember?"

"Yeah." As Gerald walked back toward the entrance, the prosecuting attorney came out. Gerald inquired about the missing signature.

"You can pick one up Monday if you want a signed one," the prosecutor explained, which seemed to satisfy Gerald.

"Mr. Devas," I offered my hand, "You did the right thing here. Thank you." I spoke softly, full of gratitude as we shook hands. He simply nodded in response. I doubted that he felt very comfortable standing in plain view with Gerald. Nothing else was said and we parted.

"I'm sorry I couldn't shake his hand, honey. But I just couldn't," Gerald professed. I told him I fully understood. We kept walking toward the exit. "That's it, huh, after all that?

After all that, that's it?" He mumbled his sentiments several times.

I felt like we should have been jumping up and down or dancing in the streets, but we weren't. I think we were still dazed and could not believe the ordeal had finally ended.

After we got home, Gerald crawled into bed, since he was suffering from another cold. I returned to work. My coworkers smiled and sensed how happy I was. They didn't really know the details, but I explained that justice was served and that Ger and I were one major step closer to getting our kids back.

I couldn't wait to get home. I spent the evening on the telephone letting family and friends know that the worst was over. We were free again.

They were all so happy for us, and they were all so loving and strong to stand by us. We planned a party for the following Saturday night.

I realized how lucky we had been in one sense. We had somehow managed to avoid being publicly outcast or branded by the entire sordid ordeal. I remembered some of the articles I had read about several falsely accused people who did not survive the lingering overt persecutory shame.

Our household immediately felt light-hearted again, more carefree, the way it used to be. As the radio played, I found myself singing along to music again, something that I hadn't done in a long time.

I spent Sunday morning privately thanking God. We sat around in the afternoon and laughed as we watched an episode of "Leave it to Beaver." Gerald was feeling better, and it was a beautiful day, so we took a drive toward evening. We spotted a scarlet tanager and red-headed woodpecker. It felt great to be able to enjoy things again, without worrying about the charges. I amused myself with the thought that Gerald was as free as a bird. He could continue to be a father and grandfather.

I left it up to him to call his sisters and kids and give them the good news. Somehow we had survived. It was incredibly comforting to know that our lives would not be further trampled upon. Tomorrow I'll buy a roll of film and take a bunch of pictures of various American flags, I thought to myself. I

186

contemplated sending the prosecuting attorney a dozen roses, but refrained. I was overwhelmed by a sense of joy and inner peace. The nagging restlessness was finally gone.

After Gerald hung up the phone, we sat across from each other at the kitchen and smiled. "I don't know, Karrol. I don't know."

"What? What?" I wondered what he was thinking.

"Maybe it's only my imagination, I don't know, but I keep thinking that the boys are going off in a room somewhere and giving each other high fives. You know? Maybe?"

"Who knows, honey, maybe. I know they love you very much, and some day they'll know just how much you love them."

"Yeah," he said softly. "Yeah, I hope so."

Life seemed so much easier after that day. I could detect the difference in Gerald, a boost in his self-esteem. The summer days got long and hot, but felt great.

One evening in June, about 6 P.M., the phone rang. My sister sounded excited. "Karrol, yes hi," she said, "listen, I have to tell you something. Are you busy?"

"No, go ahead. What is it?"

"I saw the kids, little Gerry and Todd. I saw 'em yesterday. And Todd even came back today. I tried to call you last night."

"What? You're kidding. You did? Where were they?" I asked excitedly. "Wait, wait." I yelled to Gerald who was lying down on the couch reading the newspaper. "Ger, listen, Katie saw the kids." He jumped up and sat down at the kitchen table beside me.

Katie began to explain. "Remember that one aunt of theirs, who lives in the neighborhood? Well, they said they were visiting her. They were going to the corner store. I saw them coming and knew it was Todd and Gerry. I told them I'd know my nephews anywhere. Karrol, I can't believe it. They're almost as tall as me, at least a foot taller than they were."

"Oh no, really? We saw them at the hearing at the end of January. They didn't look too tall then. Wait. Let me tell Ger. He's sitting right here. I relayed the information.

Katie continued to fill me in on what had occurred. It was too difficult to keep interrupting her, so I promised Gerald I would tell him everything after I hung up. I'm certain my questions and reactions caused Gerald to anxiously await the details.

"She says the kids visited about an hour and a half. They were really happy to see her and Jonathan. She says they told Jon about things they all did together, when he was just a baby. Let's see, they really enjoyed playing with Jon and Gin. Then listen, honey, they asked all about you and me. She says they got all bright-eyed and excited as she talked about us."

"Really? You guys aren't making this up, are you?"

"No, no, of course not. This is for real and it gets even better," I reassured him. Katie said something like 'your father and Karrol love you very much and they miss you and wouldn't ever hurt you' and the boys said, 'Yep, we know that'." I waited to see Gerald's reaction regarding the remarkable statement.

"They said that? Wow. Really? All right. Good for them. What else? C'mon, tell me everything."

I tried to relay every bit of information that my sister had shared with me. She mentioned the way Todd kept poking Gerry and telling him to be quiet because they would get into trouble. Gerald heard me ask Katie over and over if the kids actually verbalized what she said or just acted like they knew their Dad had not hurt them. I told Gerald again as he asked, "The way she put it, was that they knew in their hearts and they actually said it."

"They asked about Tiger and Dad and Katie had to tell them that they were gone. She says they put their heads down and acted real sad. I guess Gerry did a lot of the talking while Todd acted worried that they would get into trouble. But Gerry said, 'What can they do? We came to visit one of our aunts'." I noticed Gerald's grin. "Oh, I know, she says they just kept talking about how they used to play catch in the back yard, and the bike rides and walks we took, and all the sports they used to play with you. You know, all their memories from our house on Sarasota Street. She asked them what they were doing on their summer vacation, and they said, "Nothing." I let out a sigh.

"Those poor guys. They need to be involved in sports," Gerald said, then added, "So they were talking about the good times we used to have, huh? What else?"

"They sure were. It's like you said, Ger, they know what happened when you guys were together, what you did, and what you didn't do. This is incredible. I mean all this time, I was thinking they had come to believe it all. Maybe I read too much on the subject, I don't know. I sure hope they know for sure. I mean, I hope they don't have any doubts, whatsoever."

Gerald seemed relieved, yet he remained somewhat skeptical. As I explained to Katie, so often before, the kids denied the abuse, then said, okay, it happened, then they would go back to denying it. Gerald was aware of this too.

But we had reason to believe that the damage done to the kids was not as extensive as I had thought. Yet, we knew the boys had suffered tremendously. Katie described to us her observation that Todd and Gerry sensed a feeling of abandonment by their father.

I said, "Sure they feel abandoned. They wonder where their dad is, the parent they used to trust, someone they thought would always be there for them. They wonder why he doesn't come for them and help expose the truth so they can begin to deal with all of their conflicts, including their anger toward Ger for being missing for so long."

"Yeah, I could sure tell they wondered where their dad was, but Karrol, I just can't emphasize enough, the way they were reaching out, you know, the way they realized that they were missing out on seeing their dad and being a part of our family. It hurt, Karrol, because it was like the kids and me, we picked up right where we left off, but I knew I probably wouldn't get to see them anymore. But sure enough, Todd came back the very next morning to see me." She continued to tell me how great it was to see the kids, and how we just had to do something to get them back.

I told Katie we would never give up, but again, it was a matter of money and hiring a good lawyer. We also worried about initiating anything while the kids were out of school, because Flora had made the comment one time that she would

189

never allow visitation again. We didn't like the idea of perhaps subjecting the kids to more uprooting, if she decided to run off with them, just to keep them away from Gerald. "Maybe she wouldn't ever do that, I don't know. Hopefully, for the sake of the kids, she'll realize that sooner or later this thing has to be resolved."

It was an emotional evening. Gerald and I were both proud of the boys for trying to concentrate on the good times that we had shared together. We both wished that we could tell them that they didn't do anything wrong. We wanted to be sure that they understood that they were innocent victims caught up in something that had gotten out of control.

Most of all though, as I laid in bed that night, missing the boys, I wanted to say to them, 'Your father will be a part of your life again, and you will get a chance to create more fond memories. We'll be a family again someday. Just wait and see.' I wrote this poem for Gerald and the boys:

A Father's Promise

Go now children
into the dark,
for you have no choice.
Stop when you see
a spectrum of colors.
There lies a happy rainbow.
Where the moon tells a secret,
where the sun shines a light,
that's where we will meet
to find our dreams.

EPILOGUE

The story you just read did not end here. In a follow-up book entitled, FINAL SAY—ADOPTIVE LOVE, which will be published in the future, more unfortunate dramatic events unfold as these false claims continue to interfere with our life, including our plans to adopt a child.

ABOUT THE AUTHOR

Karrol Karlin lives with her family in a small town in Indiana. Currently, she is working on a book about a disabled "old lady" and her right to die with dignity. The author also plans to publish a sequel to *In Parents We Trust* in the near future entitled *Final Say - Adoptive Love*. Though she works in nursing and the social service field, Karrol states, "Nowadays, more than anything else, I feel like a writer."